Interview Math

Over 60 Problems and Solutions
for Quant Case Interview Questions

LEWIS C. LIN

ALSO BY LEWIS C. LIN

Career

Be the Greatest Product Manager Ever

Interview Preparation

Case Interview Questions for Tech Companies

Decode and Conquer

The Marketing Interview

The Product Manager Interview

Secrets of the Product Manager Interview

Negotiation

71 Brilliant Salary Negotiation Email Samples

Some mathematician…said that true pleasure lies not in the discovery of truth,
but in the search for it.
LEO TOLSTOY

Published by Impact Interview, 677 120th Ave NE, Suite 2A-241, Bellevue, WA 98105.

Several fictitious examples have been used in this book; these examples involve names of real people, places and organizations. Any slights of people, places, or organizations are unintentional.

The author and publisher have made every effort to ensure the accuracy and completeness of information contained in this book. However, we assume no responsibility for errors, inaccuracies, omissions, or any inconsistency herein.

Corporations, organizations and educational institutions: bulk quantity pricing is available. For information, contact lewis@impactinterview.com.

SECOND EDITION / Fifth Printing

Lin, Lewis C.
Interview Math: Over 60 Problems and Solutions for Quant Case Interview Questions / Lewis C. Lin.

Table of Contents

CHAPTER 5 PROFITABILITY 98

CHAPTER 6 BREAKEVEN 113

CHAPTER 7 PRICE ELASTICITY 131

CHAPTER 8 LIFETIME VALUE 145

CHAPTER 9 ISSUE TREE GENERATION 157

CHAPTER 10 APPENDIX 161

WHAT'S NEXT 164

Introduction

If you are reading this book, these questions probably sound familiar.

- How many TV ads are shown in the US each day?
- Estimate annual sales for Starbucks' retail stores in the United States.
- A running shoe manufacturer sells shoes for $100 a pair. To produce each pair, the company spends $10 in materials and $5 in labor. They have 1 million dollars in monthly operating costs. If they sell 30,000 pairs a month, what is their monthly profit?

Yes, it is those dreaded quantitative case interview questions. I call them "interview math" questions. You will find this category of questions at consulting, finance, and programming job interviews. And given our increasingly data-driven world, you will also find interview math questions at the most unlikely of places including marketing, operations and support job interviews.

After hearing a dreaded interview math question, the following thoughts might be shivering their way down your spine:

- Is this question for real?
- What are they looking for?
- How do I start?
- Did I get the right answer?

If you are looking for answers, you have found the right place. *Interview Math* will tell you what the interviewer is looking for and how to handle these questions. And best of all, you will have over 60 practice problems, along with answers to every single one of them. If you successfully complete every single practice problem in the book, you will be well on your way in handling these questions with aplomb and ease.

How to Get the Most Out of this Book

Many of you will appreciate that *Interview Math* has sample answers to quantitative interview questions. You will not find these answers anywhere else. However, do not get tempted into reading the answers as if you were reading a novel!

Instead, when you reach the practice questions, I recommend that you:

- Try solving the question(s) on your own
- Then compare your response with the sample answer

By doing so, you will get comfortable answering questions that most candidates find difficult. You will also absorb the concepts more deeply. And you will create an efficient feedback learning loop where you will deduce where your response came up short and where it surpassed the sample answer.

Find Practice Partners

Interview Math exercises are intended for self-study. Do note that interviewing is not a one-person activity and practicing with others will:

- Give you a fresh perspective
- Provide moral support
- Keep you accountable

To make it easy to connect with others who are preparing for quant case interview questions and interviews in general, I've created a special Slack community for all of you. To get an invitation, enter the following in your Internet browser: bit.ly/lewis-lin-int-community and follow the instructions to find an interview partner.

Here's what people have said about our interview practice partner community:

"Thanks for starting this community. It's pretty awesome." – A.P.

"Hey Lewis, you already know this, but you've built something amazing here. I've done a few practice interviews now and most folks have been welcoming and helpful. You should be proud ☺ Congrats." – S.G.

"Hey Lewis, awesome group you got going here! A few of us loved your presentation at Berkeley Haas this past weekend and will be using your resources to get a few study groups together to work on cases. Looking forward to interacting with everyone here." – J.Z.

One More Thing

I am always interested in hearing from readers. To send a note, ask a question or report typos just email lewis@impactinterview.com.

Lewis C. Lin

Chapter 1 The Quantitative Interview

Introduction

What is the quantitative interview?

The quantitative case interview, or interview math for short, is an interview question that tests a candidate's mathematical and logical problem-solving capabilities.

Most candidates are more comfortable with traditional interview questions such as "Tell me about yourself," "Why do you want to join our company" and "Tell me a time when you disagreed with a co-worker." But almost all candidates find interview math problems difficult to solve.

What are some examples of quant interviews?

Interview math can vary in their subject matter and difficulty. However, the most common interview math questions include market sizing, revenue estimate, and lifetime value analyses. I have included some examples below:

Category	Example
Market sizing	Estimate the total industry-wide sales of lipstick in the U.S.
Revenue estimate	Estimate annual sales for Starbucks' retail stores in the United States.
Breakeven	A running shoe manufacturer sells shoes for $100 a pair. To produce each pair, the company spends $10 in materials and $5 in labor. They have 1 million dollars in monthly operating costs. If they sell 30,000 pairs a month, what is their monthly profit?
Price elasticity	The price of a one-way ticket from Seattle to New York is $400. Should JetBlue raise the price to $450?
Lifetime value	What is the customer lifetime value of an AMEX cardholder over the next three years?

What companies and roles can I expect the quantitative interview?

In the past, these kind of interview questions were reserved for folks in hard, quantitative disciplines like financial analysts and software engineers.

However, I am now seeing these interview questions for jobs not known to be quantitative-heavy such as marketing, general management, and customer support. Here is a list of representative companies and functions where interview math questions have been asked during the job interview process:

Job Function	Sample companies
Management Consultant	McKinsey, Bain, Boston Consulting Group, Deloitte
General Management	Capital One, Taser
Marketing	General Mills, Google, Hershey, Zoosk
Software engineering	Goldman Sachs, Microsoft
Financial Analyst	American Airlines, Best Buy, JetBlue
Operations and support	Google, Yahoo
Vendor relations	Amazon, Google

Why do interviewers ask quantitative interview questions?

Interview math tests your ability to:

1. **Solve problems**. Today's business world has all sorts of new and ambiguous problems. As a professional, you will be tasked to solve problems that you may not have encountered in the past.
2. **Influence**. These days, work gets done in teams. To get all the team members marching to the same beat, a successful team member convinces others with logical, objective arguments backed by numbers.
3. **Decision-making**. The business world moves at a rapid pace, which requires professionals to act. Few can make decisions based on gut instinct like Steve Jobs. For the rest of us, we rely on data for decision-making.
4. **Numerical dexterity**. Surrounded by computers, we are accustomed to doing math with calculators and spreadsheets. As a result, we do not have as much practice calculating numbers by hand. Interview math tests your comfort when asked to manually manipulate numbers.
5. **Poise under pressure**. Good team members and leaders are poised under pressure. Poised individuals communicate, convince and lead teams with a communication approach that is balanced, not emotional. More often than not, that balanced communication approach is based on a strategy of sound logic and hard numbers.

What does the interviewer look for in an ideal response?

An ideal interview math answer has a few components:

*   **Plan of action**. Does the candidate have a clear plan of action when solving these problems?
*   **Communication skills**. Is the candidate's plan of action easy to follow?
*   **Numerical dexterity**. Does the candidate calculate numbers confidently, quickly, and accurately?
*   **Numerical interpretation**. Can the candidate use the calculations to make conclusions, and if needed, decisions?

Chapter 2 Abbreviations, Terms, and Equations

Abbreviations in the Book

This book will deal with large numbers in the thousands, millions, and billions. To save space, I will use the following abbreviations:

- K = thousands
- M = millions
- B = billions

For instance, 10K refers to 10,000. 10M is equivalent to 10,000,000, and 10B is equivalent to 10,000,000,000.

I will also use these shorthand abbreviations:

- Q = quantity
- P = price
- R = revenue
- C = cost

Also, I will refer to Q_0 as the initial quantity and P_0 as the initial price.

Terms, Concepts, and Equations

Breakeven Analysis

Breakeven analysis determines the point where incoming revenue equals the outgoing costs. The breakeven equation is as follows:

$$Breakeven = \frac{Total\ Fixed\ Costs}{Contribution\ Margin\ Per\ Unit}$$

Capital Expenditures

Refers to a business expense intended to create a future benefit.

Also known as capital expense or CAPEX, CAPEX is contrasted with operational expenditures, which are ongoing costs to run a business or product.

Churn Rate

The annual rate at which existing customers stop having a relationship with a company.

For example, if a mobile telecommunications operator loses 10% of its customers to a competitor each year, their churn rate is 10%.

Contribution Margin ($)

This is the product's selling price minus its variable costs. In equation form, this is represented as follows:

$$Contribution\ (\$) = Price - Variable\ Cost$$

Contribution margin is different from gross margin, which includes allocated overhead.

Contribution Margin (%)
This is contribution margin represented as a percentage. In equation form, this is defined as:

$$Contribution\ Margin\ (\%) = \frac{Contribution\ Margin\ (\$)}{Price}$$

Costs
Costs refer to the cost of running a business, defined in two components: fixed and variable costs. In equation form, total cost is defined as follows:

$$Costs = Fixed\ Costs + Variable\ Costs$$

Cost of Goods Sold
This is the cost of producing goods sold by a company. It could include the cost of materials and labor to produce the goods. Cost of goods sold can also include allocated overhead.

Customer Lifetime
This is the duration for which a customer has a relationship with an employee, where the company presumably generates revenue from that customer relationship.

Customer lifetime can be calculated using the following equation:

$$Customer\ lifetime = \frac{1}{Customer\ churn\ rate}$$

Examples:

- If monthly customer churn rate is 5%, then customer lifetime is 1/5% = 20 months.
- If annual customer churn rate is 15%, then customer lifetime is 1/15% = 6.67 years.

Customer Lifetime Value
Total profit a company generates from a single customer's lifetime. The equation for calculating lifetime value is as follows:

$$Lifetime\ value = Average\ customer\ contribution\ margin\ (\$)\ per\ year * Customer\ lifetime$$

Examples:

- If a customer's average contribution margin ($) is $100 annually and customer lifetime = 5 years, then lifetime value = $500.
- If an average customer purchase is $100 annually and the contribution margin is 20%, then the average customer contribution is $20 annually. If the churn rate is 10%, then the average customer lifetime is 10 years. The lifetime value is then $20 * 10, or $200.

Here's another way to calculate customer lifetime value:

$$Lifetime\ value = Average\ customer\ contribution\ margin\ (\$) * \frac{Retention\ Rate}{1 + Discount\ Rate - Retention\ Rate}$$

This version factors in the time value of money by using a discount rate. Most interviewers will not expect you to calculate lifetime value with a discount rate since it is time-consuming.

Depreciation
When a capital asset has been consumed or expired, the capital asset's diminished value is considered an expense.

EBITDA
Earnings before Interest, Tax, Depreciation, and Amortization (EBITDA) is a financial metric that represents exactly what its name suggests. EBITDA is a popular way of comparing financial performance between companies. Unlike EBITDA, earnings can appear to be unreasonably low, especially if some companies make aggressive capital investments or take on higher debt loads.

Fixed Costs
Fixed costs are costs that do not change with the quantity of goods or services produced. Examples include:

- Some utilities, such as telephone and Internet
- Labor, such as manager's salaries or janitorial wages, which do not increase with the production of additional goods
- Advertising and marketing
- Insurance
- Interest
- Rent
- Depreciation

Gross Profit ($)
This is a company's remaining profit, after selling a product and subtracting the cost associated with its production and sale.

$$Gross\ Profit\ (\$) = Revenue - Cost\ of\ Goods\ Sold$$

Gross profit is different from contribution margin. Gross profit includes allocated overhead while contribution margin does not.

Gross Profit Margin (%)
This is gross profit represented as a percentage. In equation form, this is defined as:

$$Gross\ Profit\ Margin\ (\%) = \frac{Gross\ Profit\ (\$)}{Revenue}$$

Gross profit (%) is also known as "gross margin" or "gross profit margin."

Marginal Cost

The added cost of producing one extra unit of a product.

Market Penetration
Number of current customers relative to total potential customers. In equation form:

$$Market\ penetration = \frac{Current\ customers}{Total\ potential\ customers}$$

For example, if there are 320M people in the United States, and 300M people have televisions, then the penetration rate is approximately 94%.

Market Share
A product's share of all sales in that product category. For example, Coca-Cola's market share of non-alcoholic beverages has been roughly 40% in the last ten years.

Mixed Costs
Costs that have a fixed and variable cost component. For example, electricity costs vary with the amount of goods produced in aluminum and ceramics.

Net Present Value
The present value of a future set of cash flows. A cash payout in the future is considered less than the same cash payout in the present, due to the time value of money.

Net Profit ($)
Net profit is calculated by subtracting all costs from revenue. Costs include the cost of sales, overhead, taxes, and depreciation. In equation form, net profit is formally defined as follows:

$$Net\ Profit\ (\$) = Gross\ Profit - Depreciation - Amortization - Other\ Expenses - Interest - Tax$$

The shorthand equation for net profit can also be defined as:

$$Net\ Profit\ (\$) = Sales\ revenue - Total\ costs$$

Also known as net income or the bottom line.

Net Profit (%)
This is net profit ($) represented as a percentage. The equation is defined as follows:

$$Net\ Profit\ Margin\ (\%) = \frac{Net\ Profit\ (\$)}{Revenue}$$

Also known as profit margin or net profit margin.

Operating Expenditures
Refers to the ongoing cost of running a product or business. This could include fixed and variable costs.

Also known as operating expense or OPEX, OPEX is contrasted with capital expenditures, which is a business expense intended to create a future benefit.

Operating Income

Operating income is defined as follows:

$$Operating\ income = Revenue - operating\ expense$$

Operating Margin

Operating margin is the ratio of operating income over total revenues. In equation form:

$$Operating\ margin = \frac{Operating\ income}{Total\ revenue}$$

Overhead

Refers to ongoing expenses of operating a business. Examples could include fixed costs such as rent, gas, and electricity.

Payback Period

Payback period measures the number of years it will take to recover cash invested in a project.

$$Payback\ Period\ in\ Years = \frac{Initial\ Investment}{Annual\ Profit}$$

Price Elasticity

Price elasticity is a measure of how demand or supply changes when price changes. I will discuss price elasticity in more detail later in the book.

Profit

Profit is the business' gain after subtracting its costs from revenue. It is represented in equation form as follows:

$$Profit = Revenue - Costs$$

Alternatively, profit can be calculated as follows:

$$Profit = Revenue * Margin\ \%$$

Margin is a ratio that indicates how much revenue is profit. For example, Starbucks has a roughly 80% margin. That is, for every $5 latte they sell, 80% of that $5 is pure profit. The $1 that is not profit goes towards producing the good, whether it is the coffee beans, water, coffee cup, or labor to produce the latte.

To be more specific, there are two types of profit:

$$Gross\ Profit = Revenue * Gross\ Margin\ \%$$

$$Net\ Profit = Revenue * Net\ Margin\ \%$$

Retention Rate

This is a measure of current customers kept at the end of a period relative to customers available at the beginning of the period. In equation form:

$$Retention\ rate = \frac{Customers\ kept\ at\ the\ end\ of\ a\ period}{Total\ customers\ available\ at\ the\ beginning\ of\ the\ period}$$

Retention rate can also be calculated as follows:

$$Retention\ rate = 1 - Churn\ rate$$

Revenue
Revenue is sales generated for a product. For interview math questions, it is defined as:

$$Revenue = Price * Quantity$$

Price refers to a product's price, and quantity refers to quantity sold for that product.

Return on Investment
Also known as ROI, return on investment measures benefit a business receives when making an investment. In equation form:

$$ROI = \frac{Gain\ from\ an\ investment - Cost\ of\ investment}{Cost\ of\ Investment}$$

ROI is typically represented as a percentage.

Return on Sales
Return on sales, also known as ROS, is profit as a percentage of revenue. Like ROI, ROS is another profitability metric.

$$ROS = \frac{Net\ income}{Sales\ revenue}$$

Time Value of Money
The idea that money in the present is worth more than money in the future. For example, money in the present can be deposited into a savings account now, where it can earn interest, whereas money in the future cannot.

Variable Cost
Variable costs are costs that change with the quantity of goods and services produced. Examples include:

- Materials
- Direct Labor
- Sales Commission
- Packaging
- Shipping
- Depreciation, such as machine depreciation, based on machine hours used to produce each good or service

Chapter 3 Assumptions

Introduction

What are assumptions, and why is it important for interview math questions?

Assumptions refer to information that you accept as true, without proof.

An interview math question may ask you to estimate various values including revenue, customer demand, and production capacity. Your response to an estimation question will be more credible when you derive your final answer from intermediate building blocks. For example, when estimating demand for real Christmas trees, your final answer may depend on the following:

- Number of people that celebrate Christmas
- Breakdown of real vs. artificial Christmas tree purchases

During the interview, you may or may not have knowledge about Christmas tree purchases. At that point, you can try asking the interviewer. However, the interviewer may not have those values available, or he may choose not to disclose them to you. And unfortunately, most interviewers do not want you to Google search an answer on your smartphone.

Isn't it ridiculous if I cannot ask or research the assumptions?

An estimation question is meant to simulate the real world. That is, decision-makers often make decisions or recommendations based on imperfect or missing information. Faced with imperfect information, most professionals do not quit. Instead, they estimate imperfect information. Based on their best estimates, professionals will act accordingly.

Part of estimating well is having sound judgment to propose reasonable assumptions. I have typically found that those who are well-read and intellectually curious are most likely to propose reasonable assumptions. Going into the interview, it helps to read extensively, especially in the industry you are interviewing for.

How do I come up with assumptions?

There are three main ways:

1. Research critical assumptions before the interview
2. Ask the interviewer
3. Come up with your own

Research critical assumptions before the interview

The best way to come up with assumptions is by researching the assumptions you need before the interview. For example, for most management consulting interviews, knowing the population and life expectancy numbers for your home country would be helpful. In this book, you will find default assumptions for my home country, the United States.

If you are interviewing for a more specific role or industry, research the role or industry-specific stats before the interview. For instance, if you are interviewing for a digital marketing role, it would be helpful to know the following:

- CPMs (CPM = cost per thousand ad impressions)
- CPCs (Cost per click)
- CPAs (Cost per acquisition)
- Click through rates
- Conversion rates

Later in the chapter, I recommend a list of common assumptions to memorize before your quantitative interview.

Ask the interviewer

A job interview is a dialogue, not a one-way conversation. Keeping this in mind, as a candidate, you have the liberty to ask the interviewer for an assumption. Interviewers from particular companies, such as management consulting firms, expect candidates to ask for assumptions. Thus, they are often ready to answer your question or provide a hint. Interviewers from other companies may not expect you to ask, and if you try, they may not answer. Instead, they expect you to come up with your own assumption.

Either way, it does not hurt to ask. Even if the interviewer rejected your request, you would have had to provide your own assumption anyway.

Come up with your own

In most situations, coming up with your own assumptions is the default scenario. Later, I will provide tips on coming up with credible and convincing assumptions.

For assumptions or calculations, can I round numbers up or down?

With estimation questions, interviewers expect you to do your calculations by hand. No calculators or computers. When calculating numbers by hand, rounding numbers up or down makes it far easier.

However, be judicious in how you round numbers. Rounding the number of people in the United States from 319M to 320M is sensible. However, rounding 142M to 100M could be perceived as being sloppy and inattentive to detail. As a rule, attempt to round numbers by no more than 10 percent.

Lastly, let's say you're multiplying two numbers. If you're rounding the first number up, see if you can round the second number down so that the rounding effects compensate for each other.

Common assumptions to know and memorize

Here are some common assumptions that would be helpful to know and memorize before the interview.

Population: United States

United States	325M
New York City	8.6M
Los Angeles	4.0M
Chicago	2.7M
San Francisco	884K
Seattle	725K

Population: Outside the United States

World	7.7B
Europe	741M
Asia	4.5B
South America	423M
Africa	1.2B
China	1.4B
India	1.3B
Japan	127M
UK	66M

Other Useful Assumptions for the United States

Life Expectancy	80 years
People per Household	2.5 people
Median Household Income	$53K
GDP	$16.8 T
GDP Growth Rate	2%
Corporate Tax Rate	21%
Smartphone Penetration	70%
Percent with Bachelor's Degree	30%
Percent Married Adults	52%
Percent Under the Age of 18	23%
Percent Over the Age of 65	13%

Advice on coming up with your own assumptions

Here are tips on how to come up with assumptions for market share, stores in a geographic region, and pricing.

Market share or adoption

When estimating adoption or market share for a specific store, product or service, my favorite method is using what I call the Focus Group of 10. Here is how it works:

1. **Determine the assumption you need**. For example, you need to know the percent of Americans that drive a Ford.
2. **Consider that assumption with a focus group of 10 friends**. Among ten of my closest friends, only one person drives a Ford.
3. **Adjust accordingly**. Most of my friends live in the Pacific Time zone. I believe Americans living closer to Detroit, where Fords are made, are more likely to drive a Ford. To compensate for my biased sample, I will adjust my 10% estimate to 15%.

Here is another example using the Focus Group of 10 method. From personal experience, out of my 10 friends, 6 of them have iPhones. However, most of us are in the tech industry, so I am guessing the actual iPhone market share is lower, perhaps closer to 45%.

Stores in a geographic region

If you need an assumption for the number of stores in a geographic region, I would recommend the following:

1. **Clarify the needed assumption**. For example, we need the number of Starbucks stores in the United States.
2. **Find a ratio of residents per store**. For instance, based on prior research, there are approximately 8.5M people in New York City and 300 Starbucks stores. Divide 8.5M people by 300 stores to get our desired ratio: 28,300 people per store.
3. **Calculate the number of stores for the geographic region**. Continuing with the example, the United States region has approximately 320M people. Divide that number by 28,300 per store to get the desired value: 11,258 Starbucks stores in the United States.
4. **Adjust accordingly**. For example, our calculation is based on a store ratio for New York City, where customer demand for Starbucks coffee is higher and the customers' willingness to wait is lower. It is reasonable that other parts of the United States would differ from New York City. Thus, we can adjust our estimate downward from 11,258 to approximately 8,000 stores. After searching the Internet, we find that the actual number of Starbucks stores in 2014 is 7,303.

Pricing

When estimating revenue, candidates often need to know and use a product's price. However, products may sell for different prices. For example, Starbucks has over 60 items on their menu. It would be tedious to utilize the exact price for every single one of those 60 items. Just use the average selling price instead.

For example, I would assume Starbucks' average sales price to be $6. I believe this is realistic given that:

*   Starbucks' coffees can range from $1.75 to $4.95.

- Customers may also add a non-coffee item, such as a breakfast sandwich, to their purchase.
- Customers often purchase multiple items for friends, family, and co-workers.

Practice Questions

1. How many BMW dealerships are in the United States?
2. How many airports are in the United States?

BMW Dealerships

How many BMW dealerships are in the United States?

Show your work below. Make any assumptions as necessary. Answer on the next page.

Answer: BMW Dealerships

Goal
Number of BMW dealerships in the United States

Knowledge We Know Prior to the Interview
- Approximately 320M people in the United States
- Approximately 850K people in San Francisco (SF)
- One BMW dealership in SF

Critical Ratio
People per BMW dealership

Calculations

$$People\ per\ BMW\ dealership = \frac{850K\ people\ in\ SF}{1\ BMW\ Dealership\ in\ SF}$$

$$BMW\ Dealerships\ in\ the\ USA = \frac{320\ M\ people}{850\ K\ people\ per\ dealership} = 376\ dealerships\ in\ the\ USA$$

Adjustments
BMW dealerships are more popular in San Francisco, whose wealthy residents like to drive luxurious, performance vehicles. The rest of the United States do not share the same characteristics, so let us discount the number by 20% from 376 to 301.

Actual number
There were 341 BMW dealerships in the United States in 2018.

Airports

How many airports are in the United States?

Show your work below. Make any assumptions as necessary. Answer on the next page.

Answer: Airports

Goal

Number of airports in the United States

Knowledge We Know Prior to the Interview

- Approximately 320M people in the United States
- Approximately 8.3M people in New York City (NYC)
- Three airports in the NYC area: John F. Kennedy, LaGuardia and Newark International Airports

Critical Ratio

People per airport

Calculations

$$People\ per\ airport = \frac{8.3\ M\ people\ in\ NYC}{3\ airports\ in\ NYC} = 2.8\ M$$

$$Airports\ in\ the\ USA = \frac{320\ M\ people}{2.8\ M\ people\ per\ airport} = 114\ airports\ in\ the\ USA$$

Adjustments

Compared to airports in NYC, airports in the rest of the United States are much smaller. For example, JFK airport in NYC has 128 gates. Many airports in the United States that have less than ten gates.

Let us assume the average US airport has 10 gates. Thus, JFK airport is about 12.8 times bigger than the average airport. As a result, let us adjust our number by 12.8 times. Multiplying 114 airports by 12.8, the result is 1,459 airports.

Actual number

According to the CIA World Factbook, there were 15,079 airports in the United States in 2014. Possible reasons why this estimate is much larger than our estimate:

- CIA defines airport as a location with a recognizable runway, paved or unpaved, from the air.
- Airports that meet this definition include military bases, airparks, and glider ports. None of these were factored into our estimation.

Chapter 4 Estimation

Introduction

What are estimation questions?

Estimation questions test your ability to approximate a value. Here are some examples one might encounter in an interview:

- What is the market size of disposable diapers in China?
- Estimate annual sales for Starbucks' retail stores in the United States.
- Estimate summer sales of Disneyland tickets in the United States.

Some candidates refer to estimation questions by their catchier portmanteau, guesstimates.

What are the different types of estimation questions?

There are different types of estimation questions; market sizing and revenue estimations are two of the most common.

What is a market sizing question?

In the phrase "market sizing questions," "market size" refers to a total addressable market. That is, what would be a company's revenue if it had 100% market share of a category? For example, an interviewer may ask you the following market sizing estimation question: "What is the market size of disposable diapers in China?"

Market size is usually stated in terms of revenue, but some interviewers may define it in terms of units sold. To minimize miscommunication, clarify with the interviewer.

Examples of market sizing questions include:

- What is the market size of women's rain boots in Seattle?
- What is the market size of toothbrushes in the United States?
- What is the market size of real Christmas trees in the United States?

What is a revenue estimation question?

For revenue estimations, a candidate is expected to calculate company, product, or service revenues.

Examples of revenue estimation questions include:

- Estimate annual sales for Subway restaurants in the United States.
- Estimate annual sales of Target's brick-and-mortar stores in the United States.
- Estimate annual sales of Netflix online streaming subscriptions in the United States.

Why do interviewers ask these questions?

Interviewers use estimation questions to evaluate a candidate's:

- **Problem-solving skills**. Can a candidate take an unfamiliar problem and develop a plan to solve it confidently?
- **Communication skills**. Can the candidate clearly communicate his or her action plan to the interviewer? Is it easy-to-follow? Or does the interviewer have to ask an excessive number of clarifying questions to unravel the candidate's thoughts?
- **Analytical dexterity**. Can the candidate confidently calculate numbers in real-time? Or is the candidate hesitant? Does the candidate rely on using a calculator or computer to crunch numbers? Or does the candidate needlessly round up numbers to oversimplify calculations?
- **Judgment**. Does the candidate choose reasonable assumptions, backed by logical thinking? Or is the candidate too casual and sloppy?

Some may deride estimation interview questions as not having real-world applicability. However, estimation is a skill that helps professionals do their jobs. For example, if you are a storekeeper, your responsibilities include figuring out how much inventory to order. If you are an equity analyst, you may estimate a firm's future enterprise value.

Estimation can also help with decision-making. Here is an example: let us say we are evaluating a business decision; we want to open a new McDonald's in our city. To breakeven, we need to generate $500,000 in sales. There are several McDonalds' stores already, which means we are not going to get many customers.

Given this constraint, let us say for the sake of argument, we deduced that each visitor needs to spend $150 to breakeven. Yikes! We just identified a flaw in the investment thesis. A typical McDonald's customer spends $8; getting customers to spend $150 per visit is a big stretch. To summarize, the estimation example showed how our calculations identified a faulty sales per visitor assumption.

What are they looking for in an ideal response?

A top-notch estimation answer would include the following components:

- **Logical plan of action that is easily understood.** Interviewers want to feel confident (and you should feel confident too) that you have a clear plan when solving an ambiguous estimation problem. Good candidates communicate a plan that not only gets them to the right answer but also easy for the listener to follow along.
- **Communication skills.** Interviewers do not just want to hear the answer. They also want to understand the thinking too. Thus, candidates who silently solve a problem on their own and resurface in five minutes will not do well. Communicating one's thoughts is critical to sharing knowledge and gaining buy-in to one's approach.
- **Choose reasonable assumptions with clear explanations.** Interviewers would like you to use reasonable assumptions. Silly assumptions such as "there are 100 billion people in the world" show that a candidate is out-of-touch, which minimizes the individual's credibility with clients, executives, and co-workers. Furthermore, it would be polite to explain why you chose a specific assumption.
- **Accuracy.** Some estimations are the basis for decision-making. Thus, accuracy is important. But clearly, accuracy will improve if there is more time to work on it. Given an interview scenario, most interviewers

would like candidates to spend at most 15 minutes and as little as 5 minutes on an estimation question. Candidates must tradeoff between accuracy and speed – and get the most accurate response possible in a 10-minute timeframe.

I heard the answer is not important for estimation questions. Is that true?

Opinions on this vary. Starting with the facts:

- **Interviewers want to understand "how you think."** When interviewers utter this phrase, they are usually referring to two things:
    1. Do you have a plan of action?
    2. Can you communicate your problem-solving process in a way that is effective, efficient, and easy to follow?
- **Interviewers want to see that you are numerically savvy and detail oriented.** Many candidates are afraid to compute and sometimes, even discuss numbers. They expect candidates to talk details, do math, and do math quickly.

When candidates say, "the answer is not important," I believe what they really mean is the answer does not have to be 100 percent accurate. Yes, if a candidate is asked to estimate the Chinese diaper market, candidates do not have to say $49.9 B. However, if the interviewer has the number $50 B in his head, it would be unreasonable to arrive at $10M or $10 trillion as the final value.

So, the final takeaway is this: the *precision* of your final is not important. However, what is important is that your final answer be reasonably close, *taking into consideration* the available time to answer the question. The more time you have, the more accurate your answer should be.

How long should I spend on an estimation question?

Most interviewers expect you to finish an estimation question in less than 10 minutes, while impatient interviewers may be frustrated if you spend more than five. If you are taking over 15 minutes, you are taking too much time.

How should I approach estimation?
Market Sizing Questions

For a market sizing question, use a top-down approach. That is, start from the whole, usually population, and work your way down to the parts. Here are some questions you may want to consider as you work your way down from population:

Question	One Example	Another Example
How many people are in the population?	1.2 B people in China	319M people in the United States
What are the defining characteristics of the target customer?	Children under the age of four are likely to wear disposable diapers. Five percent of the population are four years and younger.	People that celebrate Christmas are likely to buy a real Christmas tree. 95 percent of Americans celebrate Christmas.
How often does the target customer purchase?	Parents buy diapers once a month. Children use about ten diapers per day.	Households typically buy Christmas trees once a year.
What quantity do they purchase when they do purchase?	Parents buy two boxes of diapers per month. Each box has 150 diapers.	Households typically buy one Christmas tree.
How much does each unit cost?	Each diaper costs $0.25.	Each Christmas tree costs $75.

When solving a market sizing question, here's what I visualize:

Revenue Estimation Questions

For a revenue estimation question, use a bottom-up approach. That is, start with a *single unit* and multiply by *total units* to get the whole. Here are a couple of examples:

Example 1

In this example, our desired goal is estimating Starbucks' store revenue in the United States (USA). Here is our estimation approach:

- **Step 1**. Estimate revenue for a single Starbucks' store. I refer to this above as the single unit.
- **Step 2**. Estimate the number of stores in the USA. I refer to this as total units.
- **Step 3**. Multiply the two numbers to get Starbucks' store revenue in the USA.

Example 2

In this example, our desired estimate is Disneyland's summer revenue. Here is our estimation approach:

- **Step 1**. Estimate revenue for a single summer day at Disneyland.
- **Step 2**. Estimate the number of days in the summer.
- **Step 3**. Multiply the two numbers to get Disneyland's summer revenue.

Approach for Other Estimation Questions

For other estimation questions, use the following approach:

- **Step 1.** Identify the goal.
- **Step 2.** Break the goal into components.
- **Step 3.** Solve each piece.
- **Step 4.** Aggregate all the pieces.

Of all the steps, breaking the goal into component pieces can feel intimidating. Here is a helpful tool: issue trees. Issue trees are graphical representations to break problems into component parts.

Here is an example of an issue tree:

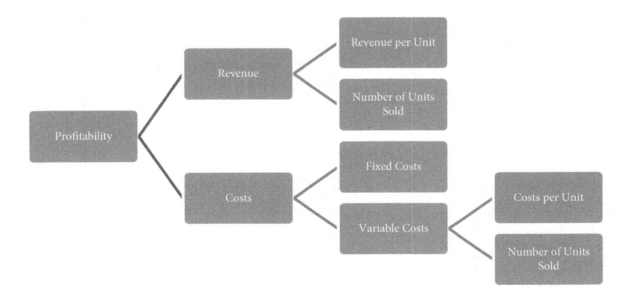

An issue tree can be drawn either horizontally or vertically.

Practice Questions, Market Sizing

1. What is the market size of disposable diapers in China?
2. What is the market size of toothbrushes in the United States?
3. What is the market size of women's rainboots in Seattle?
4. What is the market size of real Christmas (Xmas) trees in the United States?
5. What is the market size for men's dress socks in the United States?
6. How many cars cross San Francisco's Golden Gate Bridge every day?
7. Estimate the total industry sales of lipstick in the U.S.
8. What is the market size of men's haircuts in New York City?
9. How many Seattle residents have read Ayn Rand's *Atlas Shrugged* at least twice?
10. What is the market size for smartphone cases in the United States?
11. How many estimation questions will this Seattle startup ask in the next 12 months?
12. How many cars are in Los Angeles?
13. How many TV ads are shown in the US each day?

Chinese Diaper Market

What is the market size of disposable diapers in China?

Show your work below. Make any assumptions as necessary. Answer on the next page.

Answer: Chinese Diaper Market
Framework

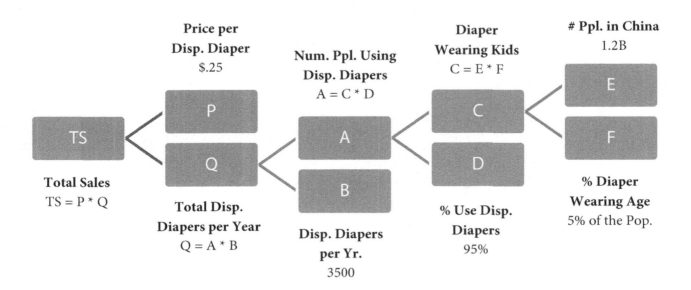

Calculations

C = 1.2B * 5% = 60M

A = 60M * 95% = 57M

Q = 57M * 3500 = 199.5B

Answer

TS = $.25 * 199.5B = $49.875B

U.S. Toothbrush Market

What is the market size of toothbrushes in the United States?

Show your work below. Make any assumptions as necessary. Answer on the next page.

Answer: U.S. Toothbrush Market

Framework

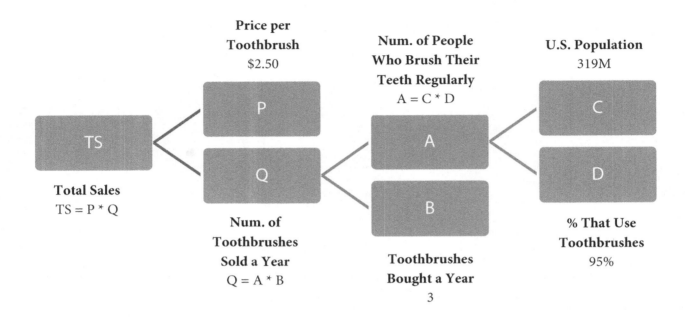

Calculations
A = 319M * 95% = 303.05M
Q = 303.05M * 3 = 909.15M

Answer
TS = $2.50 * 909.15M = $2.27B

Women's Rain Boot Market

What is the market size of women's rain boots in Seattle?

Show your work below. Make any assumptions as necessary. Answer on the next page.

Answer: Women's Rain Boot Market
Framework

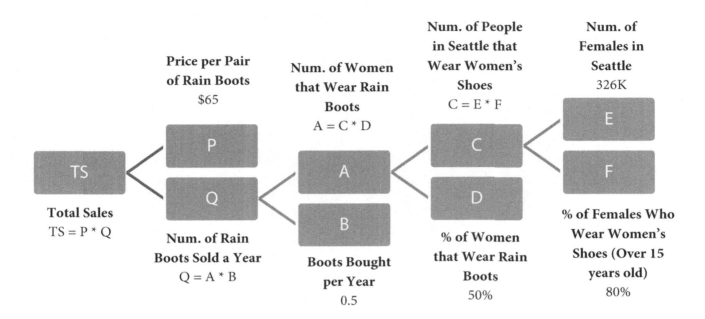

Assumptions

F: Not all Seattle females wear women's shoes. Some are children, who wear children's shoes.

D: Out of a focus group of ten Seattle women, about half wear rainboots.

B: Rain boots get replaced about once every two years.

P: Women's rain boots range from $20 to $150, with most near the middle of the range.

Calculations

E = 652K / 2 = 326K

C = 326K * 80% = 260,800

A = 260,800 * 50% = 130,400

Q = 130,400 * .5 = 65,200

Answer

TS = $65 * 65,200 = $4,238,000

U.S. Christmas Tree Market

What is the market size of real Christmas (Xmas) trees in the United States?

Show your work below. Make any assumptions as necessary. Answer on the next page.

Answer: Christmas Tree Market

Framework

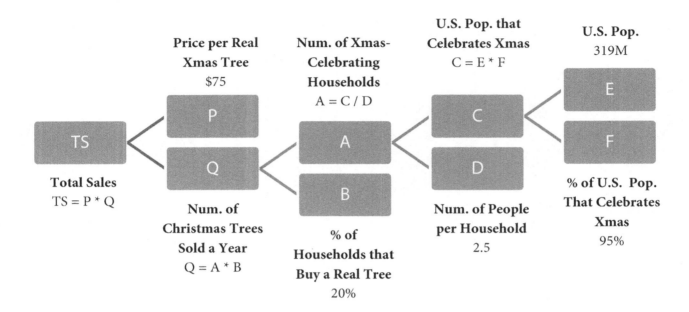

Assumptions

F: 95% of Americans celebrate Christmas. Source: Gallup/USA Today poll, Dec. 10 to 12, 2010, n = 1,019.

Calculations

C = 319M * 95% = 303.05M

A = 303.05M / 2.5 = 121.22M

Q = 121.22M * 20% = 24.244M

Answer

TS = $75 * 24.244M = $1.8183B

U.S. Dress Sock Market

What is the market size for men's dress socks in the United States?

Show your work below. Make any assumptions as necessary. Answer on the next page.

Answer: U.S. Dress Sock Market

Framework

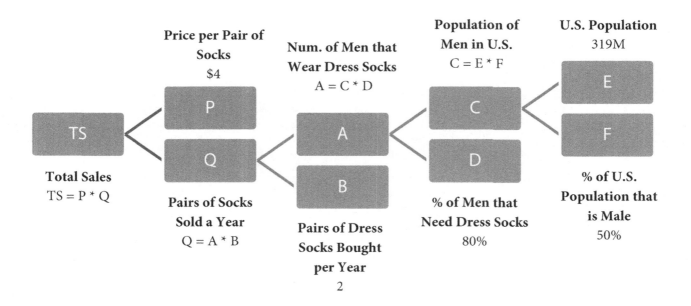

Calculations

C = 319M * 50% = 159.5M

A = 159.5M * 80% = 127.6M

Q = 127.6M * 2 = 255.2M

Answer

TS = 255.2M * $4 = $1.02B

Golden Gate Bridge

How many cars cross San Francisco's Golden Gate Bridge every day?

Show your work below. Make any assumptions as necessary. Answer on the next page.

Answer: Golden Gate Bridge

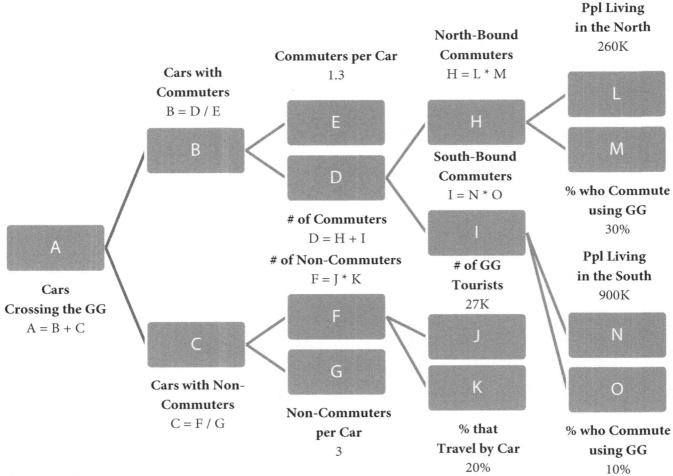

Assumptions

Commuter assumptions

- The Golden Gate Bridge (GG) connects Marin County in the North and the greater San Francisco region in the South.
- Assume 260k live in Marin County (the "North").
- Assume 900k live in the greater San Francisco region (the "South").
- Many people who live in the North are retirees. Assume that only 30 percent commute across the GG.
- Many people who live in the South don't commute into Marin, given the relatively fewer companies based there. Assume only 10 percent of those in the south commute across the GG.
- Assume 1.3 commuters per car, which doesn't include public transit.

Tourist assumptions

- The Golden Gate bridge website states 10M visitors a year, which is roughly 27K visitors per day.
- Tourists can enjoy the GG in different ways: walking, biking, or riding a tour bus.
- Assume only 20% enjoy the GG by car.
- Assume there are three tourists per car.

Other assumptions

- Non-commuters are defined as tourists.
- We will not consider commercial vehicles such as shipping trucks and public buses.
- A car that makes a round trip is considered one car. We are not considering cars that only make a one-way journey across the GG.

Calculations

- H = L * M = 260K * 30% = 78K
- I = N * O = 900K * 10% = 90K
- D = H + I = 78K + 90K = 168K
- B = D / E = 168K / 1.3 = 129K
- F = J * K = 27K * 20% = 5.4K
- C = F / G = 5.4K / 3 = 1.8K

Answer

A = B + C = 129K + 1.8K = 130.8K cars per day*

According to Golden Gate Bridge transit operations approximately 112K vehicles cross the bridge every day

Lipstick Market

Estimate the total industry sales of lipstick in the U.S.

Show your work below. Make any assumptions as necessary. Answer on the next page.

Answer: Lipstick Market

Framework

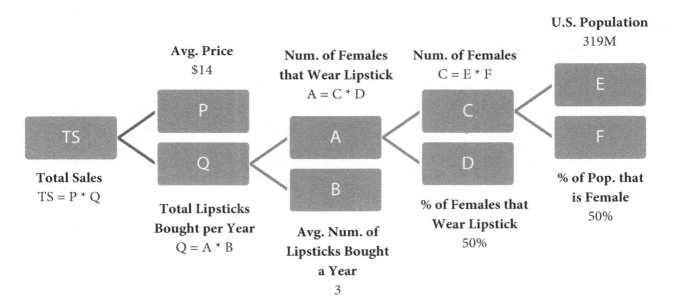

Assumptions

I am including lip gloss as well as traditional lipstick.

People who are more like to buy lipsticks are from ages 16 – 56. Given a lifespan of 80 years, the 16-56 age range, 40 years, would be 50% of the female population. I assume every female will want to own at least one pair of lipstick given heavy media exposure and influence.

There is a wide range in terms of lipstick price. I've defined the probability of purchase below as follows:

Lipstick Price (A)	Likely Target Customer (B)	% Consumers Purchasing Lipstick at this Price (C)	Expected Value (A * C = D)
$5	16-26 year olds	20%	$1.00
$10	16-26 year olds	30%	$3.00
$15	26-36 year olds	30%	$4.50
$25	26-56 year olds	20%	$5.00

Summing up the values in column D, the average price is $1 + $3 + $4.50 + $5 = $13.50, which we will round to $14.

Calculations

C = 319M * 50% = 159.5M

A = 159.5M * 50% = 79.75M

Q = 79.5M * 3 = 239.25M

Answer

TS = $14 * 239.25M = $3349.5M

New York City Haircut Market

What is the market size of men's haircuts in New York City?

Show your work below. Make any assumptions as necessary. Answer on the next page.

Answer: New York City Haircut Market

Framework

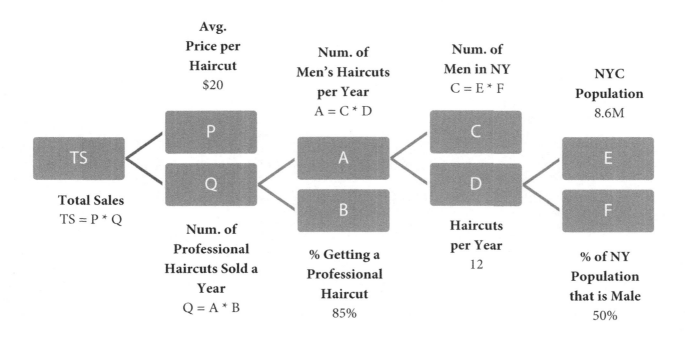

Calculations

C = 8.6M * 50% = 4.3M

A = 4.3M * 12 = 51.6M

Q = 51.6M * 85% = 43.9M

Answer

TS = $20 * 43.9M = $878M

Atlas Shrugged

How many Seattle residents have read Ayn Rand's *Atlas Shrugged* at least twice?

Show your work below. Make any assumptions as necessary. Answer on the next page.

Answer: Atlas Shrugged

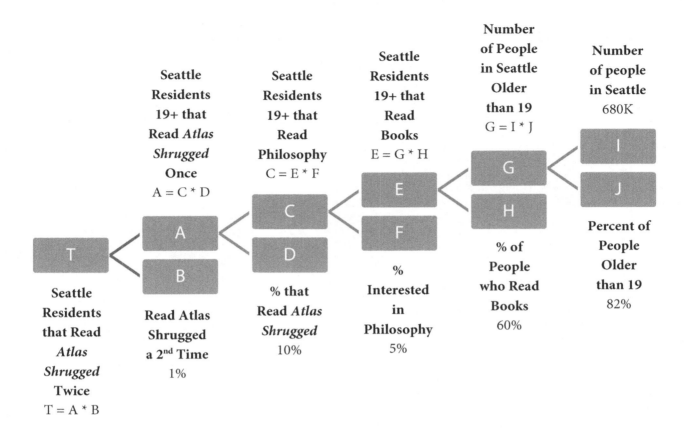

Assumptions

Assume *Atlas Shrugged* will not appeal to readers 19 years old and under.

Calculations

G = 680K * 82% = 558K

E = 558K * 60% = 335K

C = 335K * 5% = 17K

A = 17K * 10% = 1.7k

Answer

T = 1.7K * 1% = 17 Seattle Residents have Read *Atlas Shrugged* Twice

Smartphone Case Market

What is the market size for smartphone cases in the United States?

Show your work below. Make any assumptions as necessary. Answer on the next page.

Answer: Smartphone Case Market

Framework

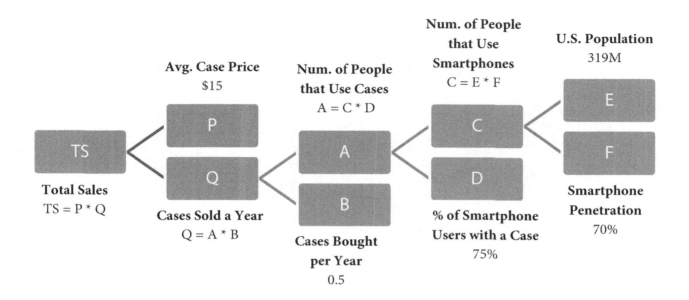

Calculations

C = 319M * 70% = 223.3M

A = 223.3M * 75% = 167.475M

Q = 167.475M * 0.5 = 83.7375M

Answer

TS = $15 * 83.7375M = $1.26B

Startup Interview Questions

A promising Seattle startup consistently asks estimation questions during the interview.

How many estimation questions will this Seattle startup ask in the next 12 months?

Assume the following:

- Eight candidates per open role.
- Hiring 20 people in the next 12 months.
- 60% of the open roles are for engineering (Eng). 10% are for product management (PM). 30% are for other roles.
- Estimation questions make up 20% of all questions asked in PM interviews, while they make up 10% of questions asked in Eng interviews and 5% of questions asked in interviews for other roles.

Show your work below. Make additional assumptions as necessary. Answer on the next page.

Answer: Startup Interview Questions

Engineering

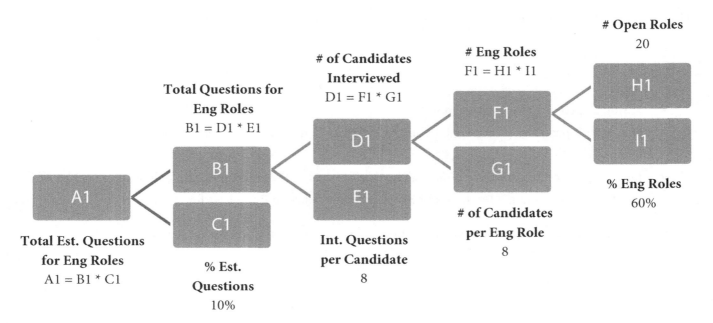

 # Open Roles
20

# of Candidates Interviewed
D1 = F1 * G1

 # Eng Roles
F1 = H1 * I1

Total Questions for Eng Roles
B1 = D1 * E1

H1

I1

F1

D1

G1

B1

C1

A1

Total Est. Questions for Eng Roles
A1 = B1 * C1

E1

% Est. Questions
10%

Int. Questions per Candidate
8

# of Candidates per Eng Role
8

% Eng Roles
60%

Product Management

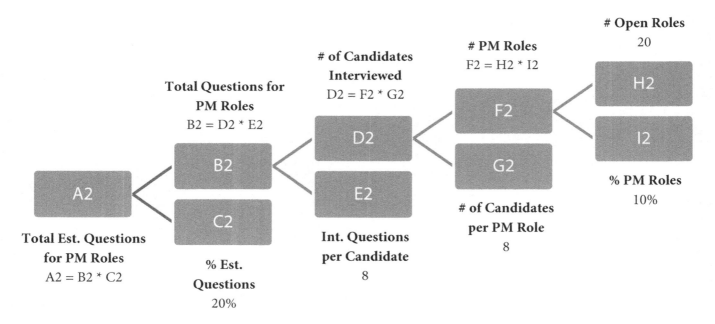

 # Open Roles
20

# of Candidates Interviewed
D2 = F2 * G2

 # PM Roles
F2 = H2 * I2

Total Questions for PM Roles
B2 = D2 * E2

H2

I2

F2

D2

G2

B2

C2

A2

Total Est. Questions for PM Roles
A2 = B2 * C2

E2

% Est. Questions
20%

Int. Questions per Candidate
8

# of Candidates per PM Role
8

% PM Roles
10%

Other

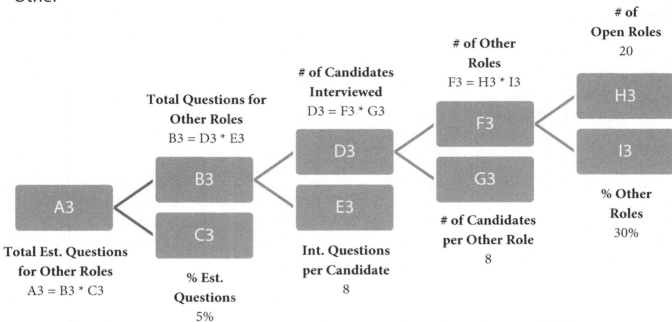

# of Open Roles
20

# of Other Roles
F3 = H3 * I3

# of Candidates Interviewed
D3 = F3 * G3

H3

Total Questions for Other Roles
B3 = D3 * E3

F3

I3

B3

D3

G3

A3

C3

E3

% Other Roles
30%

Total Est. Questions for Other Roles
A3 = B3 * C3

# of Candidates per Other Role
8

% Est. Questions
5%

Int. Questions per Candidate
8

(Answer continues on the next page)

Calculations

Engineering

- $F1 = 20 * 60\% = 12$
- $D1 = 12 * 8 = 96$
- $B1 = 96 * 8 = 768$
- $A1 = 768 * 10\% = 76.8$

PM

- $F2 = 20 * 10\% = 2$
- $D2 = 2 * 8 = 16$
- $B2 = 16 * 8 = 128$
- $A2 = 128 * 20\% = 25.6$

Other

- $F3 = 20 * 30\% = 6$
- $D3 = 6 * 8 = 48$
- $B3 = 48 * 8 = 384$
- $A3 = 384 * 5\% = 19.2$

Answer

Total Estimation Questions Asked = A1 + B1 + C1 = 76.8 + 25.6 + 19.2 ~ 122

Cars in Los Angeles

How many cars are in Los Angeles?

Show your work below. Make any assumptions as necessary. Answer on the next page.

Answer: Cars in Los Angeles (LA)

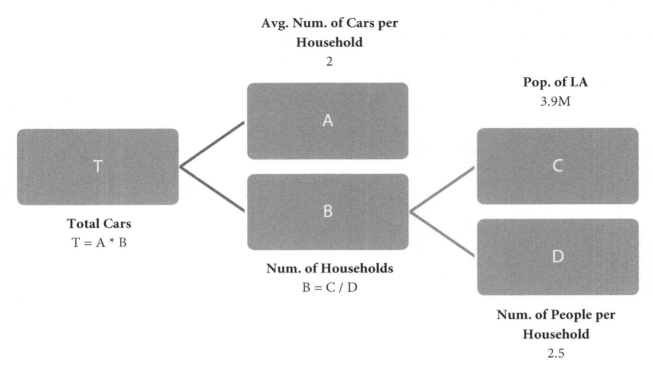

Avg. Num. of Cars per Household
2

Pop. of LA
3.9M

A

Total Cars
$T = A * B$

B

C

D

Num. of Households
$B = C / D$

Num. of People per Household
2.5

Assumptions

- Calculate for consumer vehicles only. That is, do not consider commercial vehicles or rental cars.
- Assume Los Angeles refers to the city, not the county.

Calculations

$B = 3.9M / 2.5 = 1.56M$

Answer

$T = 2 * 1.56M = 3.12M$

TV Ads

How many TV ads are shown in the US each day?

Show your work below. Make any assumptions as necessary. Answer on the next page.

Answer: TV Ads

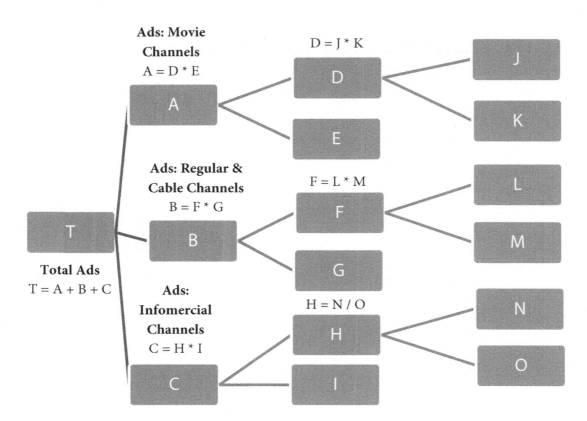

Legend

- D, F, H: Daily Ads per Channel
- E, G, I: Number of Channels (50, 500, 5)
- J: Ads per Movie (10)
- K: Num. of Movies per Day (12)
- L: Ads per TV Show (15)
- M: Num. of Shows per Day (36)
- N: Minutes in a Day (1440)
- O: Length of Infomercial Ad in Minutes (5)

Calculations

- D = 10 * 12 = 120
- A = 120 * 50 = 6,000
- F = 15 * 36 = 540
- B = 540 * 500 = 270,000
- H = 1440 / 5 = 288
- C = 288 * 5 = 1,440

Answer

T = 6,000 + 270,000 + 1,440 = 277,440

Practice Questions, Revenue Estimation

1. Estimate annual sales for Starbucks' retail stores in the United States.
2. How much does an Uber driver earn per day?
3. Estimate summer sales of Disneyland tickets in the United States.
4. Estimate annual sales of NFL tickets in the United States.
5. Estimate annual sales of Pillow Pets in the United States.
6. Estimate annual sales of Netflix online streaming subscriptions in the United States.
7. Estimate annual sales for Subway restaurants in the United States.
8. How much money does Electronic Arts' make from selling the popular Madden NFL football game?
9. How much monthly revenue does Spotify generate from their student service in the U.S.?
10. Estimate annual sales of Major League Baseball (MLB) tickets in the United States.

Starbucks' Sales

Estimate annual sales for Starbucks' retail stores in the United States.

Show your work below. Make any assumptions as necessary. Answer on the next page.

Answer: Starbucks' Sales

Framework

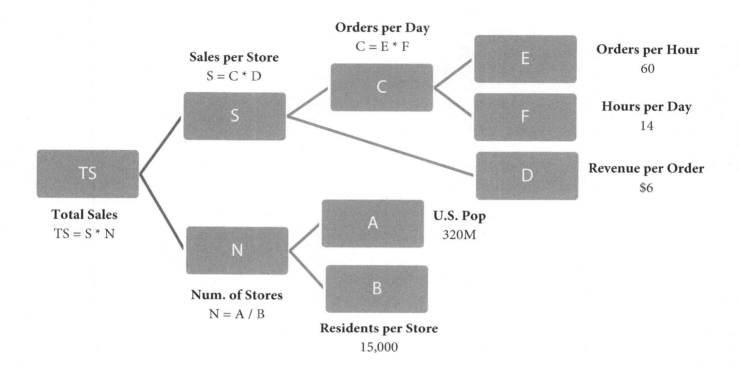

Calculations

C = 60 * 14 = 840

S = 840 * $6 = $5,040

N = 320M / 15K = 21,333

S = C * D * 365 = 840 * 6 * 365 = $1,839,600

Answer

TS = $39.2B

Uber Driver Earnings

How much does an Uber driver earn per day?

Show your work below. Make any assumptions as necessary. Answer on the next page.

Answer: Uber Driver Earnings

Trip Revenue

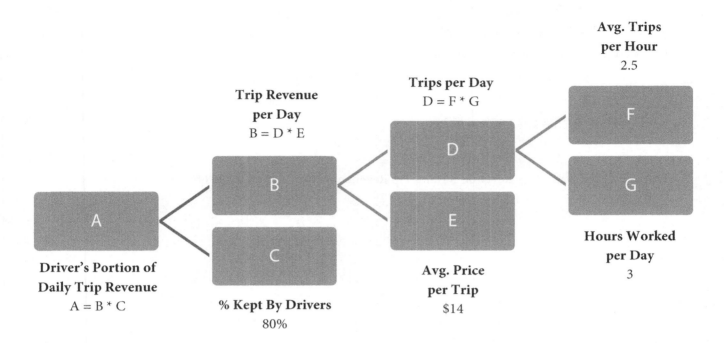

Tip Revenue

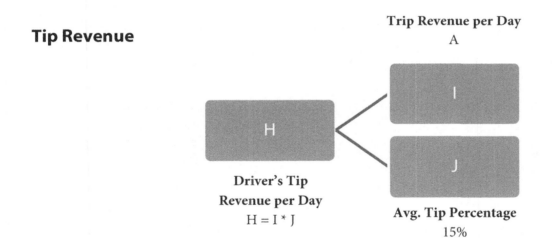

Assumptions

- Average price per trip is $14.
- Each driver does between two to three trips per hour, so we'll use an average of 2.5 trips per hour.
- According to a recent Uber driver survey, most drive 1 to 5 hrs. a week. So, we'll choose an average of 3 hours per day.
- Assume the average tip percentage is 15%. Drivers do not share the tip with the ridesharing company.
- Set aside costs, such as gas and insurance.

Calculations

Trip Revenue

- $D = F * G = 2.5 * 3 = 7.5$
- $B = D * E = 7.5 * \$14 = \$105$ per day
- $A = B * C = \$105 * 80\% = \$84$ per day

Tip Revenue

- $H = I * J = A * J = \$84 * 15\% = \$12.60$

Answer

T = Driver's Cut of Daily Trip Revenue + Daily Tip Revenue = \$84 + \$12.60 = \$96.60

Disneyland's Ticket Sales

Estimate summer sales of Disneyland tickets in the United States.

Show your work below. Make any assumptions as necessary. Answer on the next page.

Answer: Disneyland's Ticket Sales
Framework

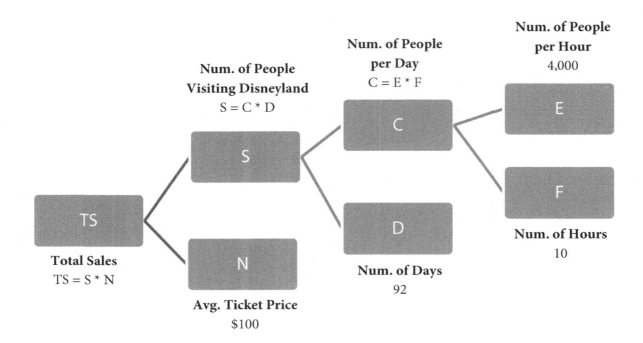

Calculations
C = 4,000 * 10 = 40,000

S = 40,000 * 92 = 3.68M

Answer
TS = 3.68M * $100 = $368M

NFL Ticket Sales

Estimate annual sales of NFL tickets in the United States.

Show your work below. Make any assumptions as necessary. Answer on the next page.

Answer: NFL Ticket Sales

Framework

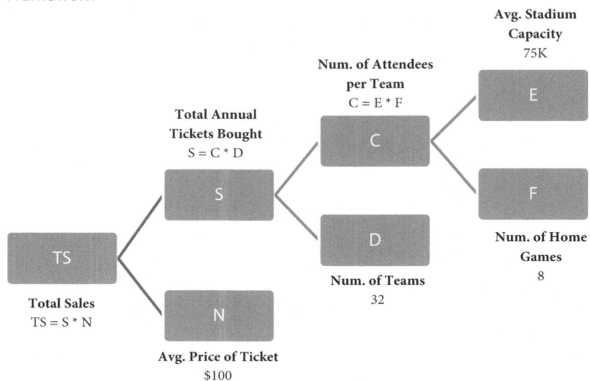

Avg. Stadium Capacity 75K

Num. of Attendees per Team C = E * F

Total Annual Tickets Bought S = C * D

E

C

F

S

D

Num. of Home Games 8

TS

Num. of Teams 32

Total Sales TS = S * N

N

Avg. Price of Ticket $100

Calculations

C = 75K * 8 = 600K

S = 600K * 32 = 19.2M

Answer

TS = 19.2M * $100 = $1.92B

Pillow Pet Sales

Estimate annual sales of Pillow Pets in the United States.

Pillow Pets is a decorative pillow that can be converted into a stuffed animal. It is popular with kids under the age of 18.

Screenshot / Pillow Pets

Show your work below. Make any assumptions as necessary. Answer on the next page.

Answer: Pillow Pet Sales

Framework

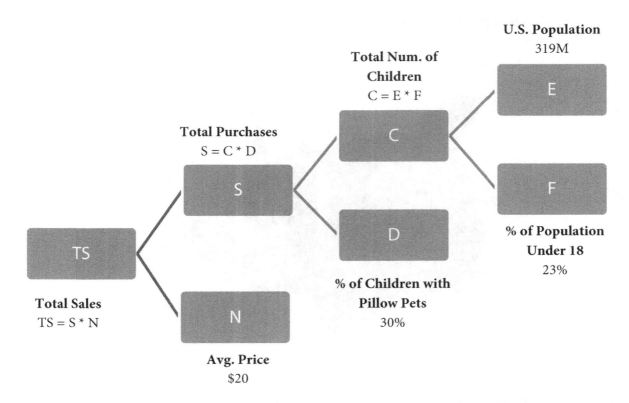

Calculations

C = 319M * 23% = 73.37M

S = 73.37M * 30% = 22.011M

Answer

TS = 22.011M * $20 = $440.22M

Netflix Subscription Sales

Estimate annual sales of Netflix online streaming subscriptions in the United States.

Show your work below. Make any assumptions as necessary. Answer on the next page.

Answer: Netflix Subscription Sales

Framework

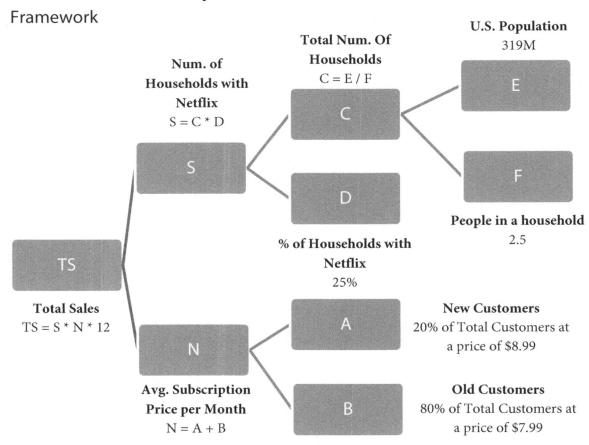

Assumptions

- A & B: In 2014, Netflix raised the price of their standard streaming-only plan from $7.99 to $8.99. However, existing customers could keep their $7.99 price for two more years. Assume that 80% of their current customers are grandfathered into the $7.99 price. Consider only their standard plan, not other plans.
- S & C: The result for S is a little below Netflix's guidance. Netflix reports there were approximately 58M US Netflix customers in 2018. Increase the % of households with Netflix assumption to close the gap with their most recently reported number.

Calculations

C = 319M / 2.5 = 127.6M
S = 127.6M * 25% = 31.9M
N = (20% * $8.99) + (80% * $7.99) = $8.19

Answer

TS = 31.9M * $8.19 * 12 = $3.14B

Target Store Sales

Estimate annual sales of Target's brick-and-mortar stores in the United States.

Show your work below. Make any assumptions as necessary. Answer on the next page.

Answer

Framework

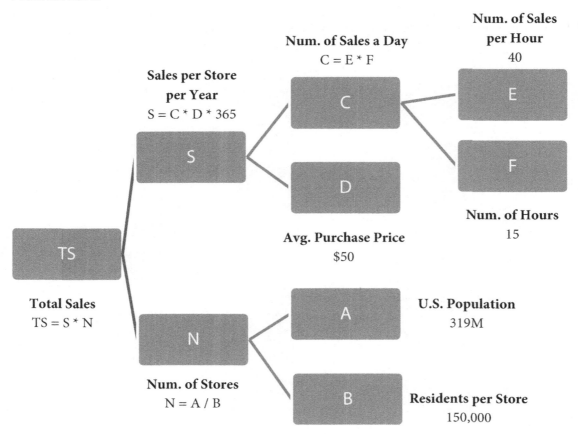

Assumptions

This calculation factors in brick-and-mortar, and not online, sales.

Calculations

C = 40 * 15 = 600

S = 600 * $50 * 365 = $10.95M

N = 319M / 150,000 = 2,126.67 = 2,127

Answer

TS = $10.95M * 2,127 = $23.29B

Subway's Sales

Estimate annual sales for Subway restaurants in the United States.

Show your work below. Make any assumptions as necessary. Answer on the next page.

Answer: Subway's Sales

Framework

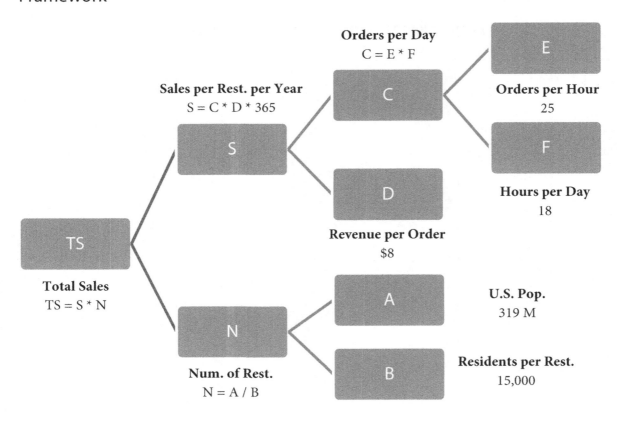

Orders per Day
C = E * F

Sales per Rest. per Year
S = C * D * 365

E

Orders per Hour
25

C

F

S

D

Hours per Day
18

TS

Revenue per Order
$8

Total Sales
TS = S * N

A

U.S. Pop.
319 M

N

B

Residents per Rest.
15,000

Num. of Rest.
N = A / B

Calculations

C = 25 * 18 = 450

S = 450 * $8 * 365 = 1.314M

N = 319M / 15,000 = 21,267

Answer

TS = $1.314M * 21,267 = $27.94B

Football Video Game

How much money does Electronic Arts' make from selling the popular Madden NFL football game?

Show your work below. Make any assumptions as necessary. Answer on the next page.

Answer: Football Video Game

Framework

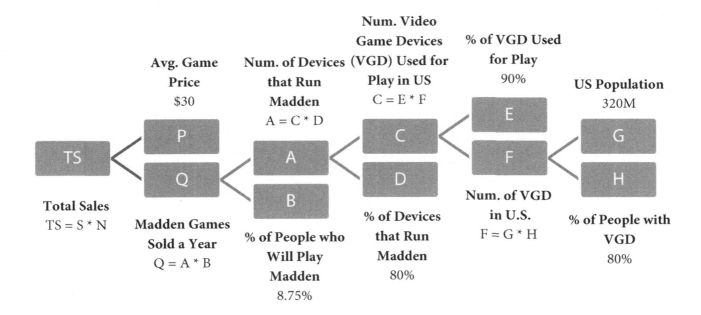

Assumptions

B: Assume that not all owners of devices that run Madden will play Madden. Let us break this down into age demographics. Assume that the life expectancy is 80 years, with people evenly distributed into ten-year brackets with about 40M people in each bracket. Using the column B assumptions below, we get 28M as the # of people that play Madden. Divide that by a total population of 320M, we get 8.75%

Age Bracket	# of People in That Bracket (A)	% of Bracket Play Madden (B)	# of People that Play Madden (C = A * B)
0-10 years	40M	5%	2M
11-20 years	40M	20%	8M
21-30 years	40M	25%	10M
31-40 years	40M	15%	6M
41-50 years	40M	5%	2M
51-80 years	120M	0%	0M
Total	**320M**		**28M**

H: In addition to PCs and video game consoles, people can now play video games on their smartphones.
G: We restrict our calculation to the US population.

Calculations

F = 320M * 80% = 256M

C = 90% * 256M = 230.4M

A = 230.4M * 80% = 184.32M

Q = 184.32M * 8.75% = 16.128M

Answer

TS = 16.128M * \$30 = \$483.84M

Spotify for Students

Spotify has a special service for college students. Instead of $10 per month for their premium service, it's only $5 per month.

How much monthly revenue does Spotify generate from their student service in the U.S.?

Assume the following:

- Assume 16 million college students in the U.S.
- Spotify also offers a family subscription. It's $15 per month and covers up to five users. Assume 15% of college students are on a Spotify family plan.
- Set aside password sharing and other cheating scenarios.

Show your work below. Make any assumptions as necessary. Answer on the next page.

Answer: Spotify for Students

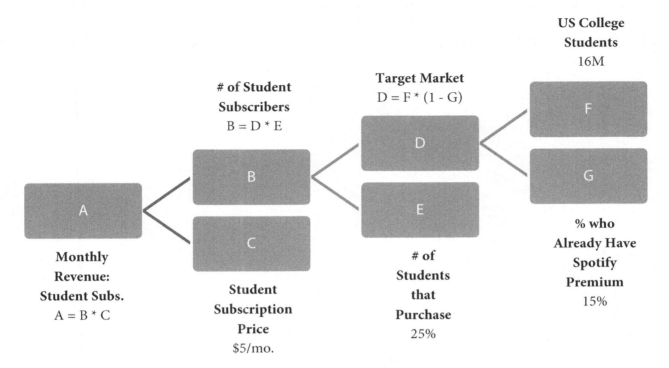

Calculation
D = 16M * (1 – 15%) = 13.6M

B = 13.6M * 25% = 3.4M

Answer
A = 3.4M * $5/mo. = $17M

MLB Ticket Sales

Estimate annual sales of Major League Baseball (MLB) tickets in the United States.

Show your work below. Make any assumptions as necessary. Answer on the next page.

Answer: MLB Ticket Sales

Regular Season

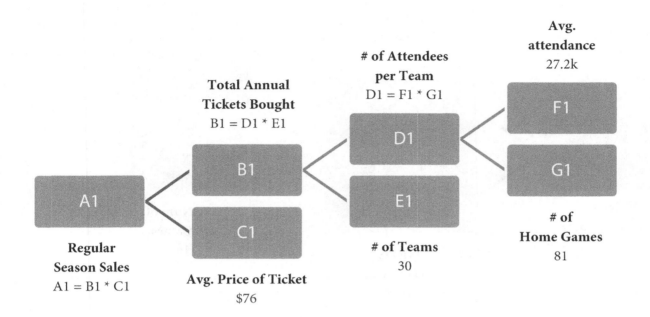

Avg. attendance
27.2k

# of Attendees per Team
D1 = F1 * G1

Total Annual Tickets Bought
B1 = D1 * E1

F1

G1

D1

B1

E1

A1

C1

Regular Season Sales
A1 = B1 * C1

Avg. Price of Ticket
$76

# of Teams
30

# of Home Games
81

Wild Card (WC)

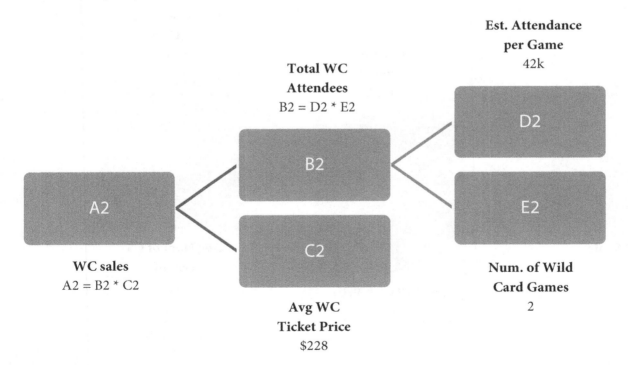

Est. Attendance per Game
42k

Total WC Attendees
B2 = D2 * E2

D2

E2

B2

C2

A2

WC sales
A2 = B2 * C2

Avg WC Ticket Price
$228

Num. of Wild Card Games
2

Divisional Series (DS)

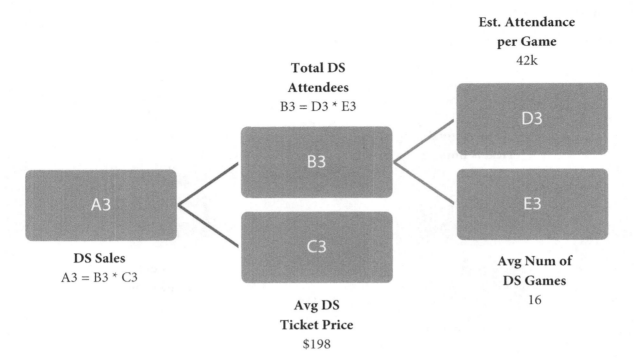

Est. Attendance per Game
42k

Total DS Attendees
B3 = D3 * E3

D3

B3

E3

A3

C3

DS Sales
A3 = B3 * C3

Avg Num of DS Games
16

Avg DS Ticket Price
$198

Championship Series (CS)

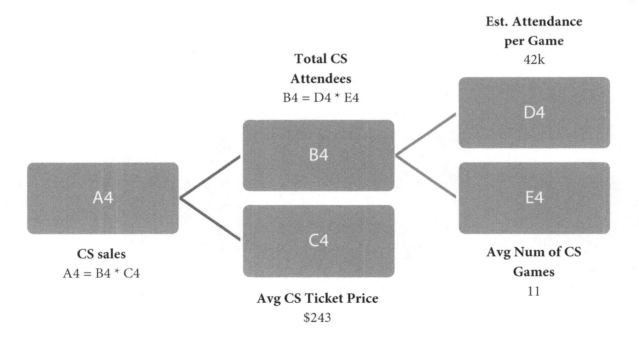

Est. Attendance per Game
42k

Total CS Attendees
B4 = D4 * E4

D4

B4

E4

A4

C4

CS sales
A4 = B4 * C4

Avg Num of CS Games
11

Avg CS Ticket Price
$243

World Series (WS)

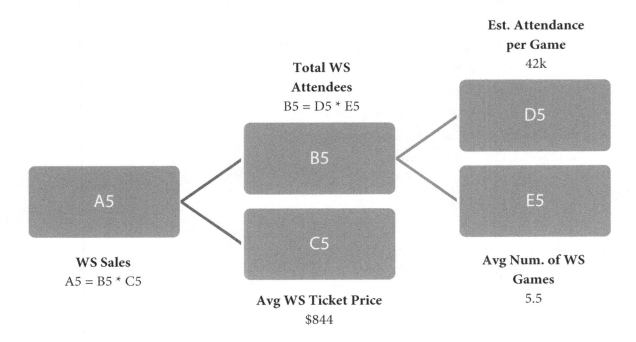

Assumptions

Regular Season

Assume the following:

- 30 teams
- 81 home games each
- $76 average ticket price
- 27,207 average attendance

Post-Season

- Number of matchups
  - Wild Card: Two matchups, one for the American League and another for the National League.
  - Divisional Series: Four matchups, consisting of four games per match.
    - Each matchup is best out of five games, meaning game matchups can be as short as three or as long as five games long. We'll go with four games for the average number of games for each Divisional Series matchup.
  - Championship Series: Two matchups, consisting of 5.5 games per match.
    - Each matchup is best out of seven games, meaning game matchups can be as short as four or as long as seven games long. 5.5 games is a reasonable assumption for the average number of games for a Championship Series matchup.

- - - o   World Series: One matchup, consisting of 5.5 games per match.
            - This matchup is also the best of seven games. Let's say 5.5 games is a reasonable assumption for the average number of games for a World Series matchup.
- - Assume average stadium capacity to be 42k; all games are sellouts.
- - Assume that post-season tickets are more expensive than the regular season:
    - o   Wild Card tickets: 3X more expensive
    - o   Divisional Series tickets: 2.6X more expensive
    - o   Championship Series: 3.2X more expensive
    - o   World Series: 11.1X more expensive

Calculations

Regular Season

$D1 = 27.2k * 81 = 2,203,200$

$B1 = 2,203,200 * 30 = 66,096,000$

$A1 = 66,096,000 * \$76 = \$5B$

Wild Card

$B2 = 42K * 2 = 84K$

$A2 = 84k * \$228 = \$19.2M$

Divisional Series

$B3 = 42K * 16 = 672K$

$A3 = 672K * \$198 = \$133M$

Championship Series

$B4 = 42K * 11 = 462K$

$A4 = 462K * \$243 = \$112.3M$

World Series

$B5 = 42K * 5.5 = 231K$

$A5 = 231K * \$844 = \$195M$

Total MLB Ticket Sales: Regular and Post-Season

Total $= A1 + A2 + A3 + A4 + A5 = \$5B + \$19.2M + \$133M + \$112.3M + 195M = \$5.46B$

Practice Questions, Geometry

1. How many leaves are on a tree?

2. Estimate the number of leaves in a leaf pile.

3. Estimate the number of golf balls that can fit in an Olympic sized pool.

Tree Leaves

How many leaves are on a tree?

Show your work below. Make any assumptions as necessary. Answer on the next page.

Answer: Tree Leaves
Formulas

- 1 cubic foot = 7.48 gallons
- Volume of a sphere = 4/3 * πr^3

Assumptions

- Assume we have a maple tree, and 150 leaves fit in a gallon container, densely packed.
- Assume the tree crown or the leafy part of the tree, is sphere-like.
- Radius of the crown is 15 feet.
- Assume the leaves, on the tree, are not densely packed. They occupy 10% of the sphere-like space.
- Assume the leaves are still on the tree; they haven't fallen due to seasonal change.

Calculations

Volume of tree crown = 4/3 * πr^3 = 4/3 * π * 15 $ft.^3$ ~ 14,137 cubic feet

Volume in gallons = 14,137 * 7.48 ~ 105,745 gallons

Leaves in gallons (densely packed) = 105,745 gallons * 150 leaves per gallon ~ 15.9M leaves

Density adjustment = 15.9M leaves * 10% = 1.59M leaves

Leaf Pile

Estimate the number of leaves in a leaf pile.

Show your work below. Make any assumptions as necessary. Answer on the next page.

Answer: Leaf Pile

Formulas

- 1 cubic foot = 7.48 gallons
- Volume of a cone = $1/3 * \pi r^2 h$

Assumptions

- Assume we have a maple tree, and 150 leaves fit in a gallon container, densely packed.
- Assume the leaf pile is cone-shaped with the following dimensions:
    - Radius of the base = 10 feet
    - Height = 2.5 feet
- Assume leaf pile is not densely packed. It occupies only 25% of the cone-like space.

Calculations

Volume of cone = $1/3 * \pi r^2 h$ = $1/3 * \pi * 10^2 * 2.5$ ~ 260 cubic feet

Volume in gallons = 260 * 7.48 ~ 1.94K gallons

Leaves in gallons (densely packed) = 1.94K gallons * 150 leaves per gallon = 291K leaves

Density adjustment = 291K leaves * 25% ~ 73K leaves

Golf Balls in a Pool

Estimate the number of golf balls that can fit in an Olympic sized pool.

Assume the following:

- An Olympic sized pool is 164 feet long, 82 feet wide, and 9.84 feet deep.
- A golf ball has a diameter of 1.68 inches.
- The golf balls can be packed to utilize space between the balls. This type of efficient arrangement allows you to pack 30 percent more balls.

Show your work below. Make any assumptions as necessary. Answer on the next page.

This is the last time I will prompt you to show your work. Keep up the good practice. And no peeking at the answer; sample answers are reserved for finishers!

Answer: Golf Balls in a Pool
Balls to fill the bottom of the pool

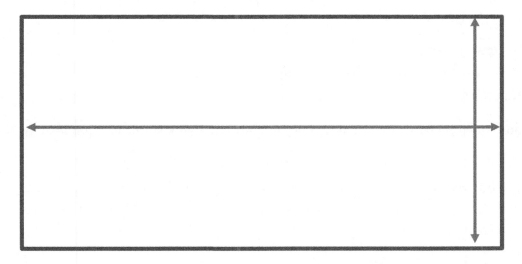

82 feet wide / 1.68 inch diameter = 585

164 feet long / 1.68 inch diameter = 1,171 golf balls

Balls to fill the bottom of the pool = Balls to fill the length of the pool * Balls to fill the width of the pool = 585 golf balls * 1,171 golf balls = 685,035 balls

Balls to fill the entire pool
Balls to fill height of the pool = Height of pool (9.84 feet) / 1.68-inch diameter = 70 balls

Balls to fill the entire pool = Balls to fill bottom of the pool * Balls to fill height of the pool = 685,035 balls * 70 balls = 47,952,450 balls ~ 48M balls.

Balls to fill the entire pool when stacking efficiently
Stacking efficiently allows us to add 30 percent more balls, which is 48M * 1.3 = 62M.

Chapter 5 Profitability

Introduction

What are profitability questions?

Profitability should be the most important business metric for any company.[1] Why would a company stay in business if it cannot generate profits?

Thus, interview math questions often center on profitability concepts and your ability to calculate profitability. Here is an example:

A manufacturer sells a specialty light bulb for $8. Material cost is $3.50. Labor cost is $2.50. Factory rent is $10,000 per month. Utilities and other operational costs are $5,000 per month. The production volume is 300,000 units per month. What is the profit per month?

Why do interviewers ask these questions?

Interviewers use profitability questions to evaluate a candidate's:

- Quantitative skills
- Understanding of business concepts
- Ability to solve ambiguous problems

What are they looking for in an ideal response?

A good answer demonstrates a candidate's:

- Understanding of profitability analysis
- Ability to explain why it is important
- Aptitude to calculate numbers quickly and use algebra

I expect top candidates to solve the following profitability problems in less than five minutes.

---

[1] There are companies where profit is not the main motivation. Reasons for this include accounting rules, an incentive to increase stock prices, and winner-take-all markets. However, we won't discuss those issues in this book. Instead, we will assume that most companies want to optimize profits.

How should I approach it?

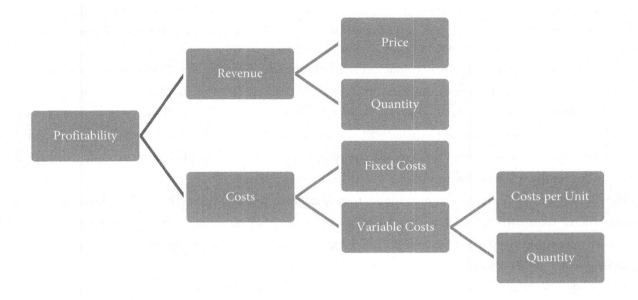

To tackle these questions, memorize the profitability tree above along with the corresponding formulas below:

- Profits = Revenue – Costs
- Revenue = Price * Quantity
- Costs = Fixed Costs + Variable Costs
- Variable Costs = Cost per Unit * Quantity

Each profitability problem will supply information that a candidate can plug into the equations above. Use basic algebra to manipulate equations to attain the desired result.

Practice Questions

1. A running shoe manufacturer sells shoes for $100 a pair. To produce each pair, the company spends $10 in materials and $5 in labor. They have 1 million dollars in monthly operating costs. If they sell 30,000 pairs a month, what is their monthly profit?

2. A manufacturer sells a specialty light bulb for $8. Material cost is $3.50. Labor cost is $2.50. Factory rent is $10,000 per month. Utilities and other operational costs are $5,000 per month. The production volume is 300,000 units per month. What is the profit per month?

3. A company sells household garden hoses for $14. Materials for each hose cost $5.50. Variable labor costs are $3.50 a hose and fixed labor costs are $2,000 a month. Factory rent is $9,000 a month. Other operational costs are $6,000 a month. The production volume is 415,000 units a month. What is their monthly profit?

4. A firm sells textbooks that are used by students across the country. They are currently selling their textbooks for $200. The cost of each book to the seller is $30. The office rent costs $10,000 a month. Other operational costs are $4,000 a month. They are selling at a volume of 3,000 a month. What is their monthly profit?

5. A Michigan company manufactures denim jeans for toddlers. Their jeans sell for $15 in local stores and $13 online on the manufacturer's website. 20% of their sales come from the local stores and 80% of their sales come from the website. Their monthly selling volume is 10,000 a month. Each pair of jeans costs the manufacturer $3 in material costs and $4 in labor costs. Their fixed costs to run the business are $8,500 a month for rent and $3,000 in other operational costs.

6. A division of a shipping company manufactures polystyrene packing peanuts. The company uses some of the packing peanuts for its own shipping but sells the rest. Each 20 cubic foot bag of packing peanuts costs the company $14 in material costs and $4 in variable labor costs. They sell each bag to customers for $27. Their monthly fixed costs include $6,000 for factory rent, $1,500 for operational costs, and $4,000 for administrative salaries. On average, the company sells 9,000 bags of packing peanuts a month. What is the company's monthly profit?

7. A New Jersey company manufactures unique, trendy hats for young adults. They sell each hat for $30 online and in their own retail stores. Each hat costs the company $7 in material costs and $5 in labor costs. The monthly fixed costs include $11,000 for rent and $5,000 in other operational costs. The company sells 12,000 hats a month. What is the company's monthly profit?

8. A Washington company sells custom pillowcases. Each pillowcase sells for $25 online. To produce each pillowcase, the company must spend $4.50 on material costs and $7 on labor costs. The company also incurs $2,500 a month on rent and $4,200 on other operating costs like equipment upkeep and advertising. If the company sells 3,000 units a month, what is their monthly profit?

9. A new company has started producing reusable water bottles. They are selling each bottle for $22 in stores and online. It costs them $7 in material costs and $5 in labor costs to make each bottle. They also have monthly fixed costs of $5,000 for factory rent, $1,500 for machine upkeep, and $3,000 for other operational costs. In month one, they sold 3,500 water bottles. They expect sales to increase by 10% every month.
    a. What is their monthly profit in month one?
    b. What is their monthly profit in month five?

10. A textile company sells towels in bulk to hotels. Each towel costs the company $4 in material costs and $2 in labor costs. The company also incurs monthly costs of $7,000 for rent and $5,000 for other operating costs. Since the towels are sold to hotels, the company sells bundles of 200 towels. Each bundle costs $1,600 and the company sells 400 bundles a month. What is their monthly profit?

Running Shoe Profits

A running shoe manufacturer sells shoes for $100 a pair. To produce each pair, the company spends $10 in materials and $5 in labor. They have 1 million dollars in monthly operating costs. If they sell 30,000 pairs a month, what is their monthly profit?

Answer

Goal
Solve for profit

Calculations
Fixed Costs (FC) = Monthly Operating Costs
FC = $1M

Variable Costs (VC) = Material Cost + Labor Cost
VC = $10 + $5 = $15

Price (P) = $100
Number Units (Q) = 30,000

Revenue (R) = P * Q = $100 * 30,000 = $3M
Costs (C) = FC + VC * Q = $1M + $15 * 30,000 = $1.45M

Answer
Profit = R – C = $3M - $1.45M = $1.55M

Light Bulb Profits

A manufacturer sells a specialty light bulb for $8. Material cost is $3.50. Labor cost is $2.50. Factory rent is $10,000 per month. Utilities and other operational costs are $5,000 per month. The production volume is 300,000 units per month. What is the profit per month?

Answer

Goal
Solve for profit

Calculations
Fixed Costs (FC) = Factory Rent + Other Operational Costs
FC = $10,000 + $5,000 = $15k

Variable Costs (VC) = Material Cost + Labor Cost
VC = $3.50 + $2.50 = $6

Price (P) = $8
Number Units (Q) = 300,000

Revenue (R) = P * Q = $8 * 300,000 = $2.4M
Costs (C) = FC + VC * Q = $15k + $6 * 300,000 = $1.815M

Answer
Profit = R – C = $2.4M - $1.815M = $585,000

Garden Hose Profits

A company sells household garden hoses for $14. Materials for each hose cost $5.50. Variable labor costs are $3.50 a hose and fixed labor costs are $2,000 a month. Factory rent is $9,000 a month. Other operational costs are $6,000 a month. The production volume is 415,000 units a month. What is their monthly profit?

Answer

Goal
Solve for profit

Calculations
Fixed Costs (FC) = Fixed Labor + Factory Rent + Other Operational Costs
FC = $2,000 + $9,000 + $6,000 = $17K

Variable Costs (VC) = Material Cost + Variable Labor Cost
VC = $5.50 + $3.50 = $9

Price (P) = $14
Number of Units (Q) = 415K

Revenue (R) = P * Q = $14 * 415K = $5.81M
Costs (C) = FC + VC * Q = $17K + $9 * 415K = $3.752M

Answer
Profit = R − C = $5.81M − $3.752 = $2.058M

Textbook Profits

A firm sells textbooks that are used by students across the country. They are currently selling their textbooks for $200. The cost of each book to the seller is $30. The office rent costs $10,000 a month. Other operational costs are $4,000 a month. They are selling at a volume of 3,000 a month. What is their monthly profit?

Answer

Goal
Solve for profit

Calculations
Fixed Costs (FC) = Rent + Other Operational Costs
FC = $10,000 + $4,000 = $14K

Variable Costs (VC) = Materials Cost
VC = $30

Price (P) = $200
Number of Units (Q) = 3,000

Revenue (R) = P * Q = $200 * 3,000 = $600K
Costs (C) = FC + VC * Q = $14K + ($30 * 3,000) = $104K

Answer
Profit = R – C = $600K – $104K = $496K

Denim Profit

A Michigan company manufactures denim jeans for toddlers. Their jeans sell for $15 in local stores and $13 online on the manufacturer's website. 20% of their sales come from the local stores and 80% of their sales come from the website. Their monthly selling volume is 10,000 a month. Each pair of jeans costs the manufacturer $3 in material costs and $4 in labor costs. Their fixed costs to run the business are $8,500 a month for rent and $3,000 in other operational costs.

   a) What is their monthly profit?
   b) The company is considering removing their jeans from the local stores and only offering online sales. As a result, the operational costs would fall to $1,500 a month. They expect selling volume to remain the same. What would be the company's monthly profit after this change? Should the company make this shift?

Answer
Part A
Goal
Solve for profit

Calculations
Fixed Costs (FC) = Rent + Other Operational Costs
FC = $8,500 + $3,000 = $11,500

Variable Costs (VC) = Materials Cost + Labor Costs
VC = $3 + $4 = $7

Store Sales Price (SP) = $15
Online Sales Price (OP) = $13
Number of Units Sold in Stores (SQ) = 20% * 10,000 = 2,000
Number of Units Sold Online (OQ) = 80% * 10,000 = 8,000

Revenue (R) = SP * SQ + OP * OQ
R = $15 * 2,000 + $13 * 8,000 = $30,000 + $104,000 = $134,000
Costs (C) = FC + VC * (SQ + OQ)
C = $11,500 + $7 * (2,000 + 8,000) = $81,500

Answer
Profit = R − C = $134,000 - $81,500 = $52,500

Part B
Goal
Solve for profit

Calculations
Fixed Costs (FC) = Rent + Other Operational Costs
FC = $8,500 + $1,500 = $10,000

Variable Costs (VC) = Materials Cost + Labor Costs

VC = \$3 + \$4 = \$7

Price (P) = \$13

Number of Units (Q) = 10,000

Revenue (R) = P * Q = \$13 * 10,000 = \$130,000

Costs (C) = FC + VC * Q = \$10,000 + (\$7 * 10,000) = \$80,000

Profit = R – C = \$130,000 – \$80,000 = \$50,000

Answer

No, the firm should not make the shift to online sales only because profit would fall by \$2,500.

Packing Peanut Profits

A division of a shipping company manufactures polystyrene packing peanuts. The company uses some of the packing peanuts for its own shipping but sells the rest. Each 20 cubic foot bag of packing peanuts costs the company $14 in material costs and $4 in variable labor costs. They sell each bag to customers for $27. Their monthly fixed costs include $6,000 for factory rent, $1,500 for operational costs, and $4,000 for administrative salaries. On average, the company sells 9,000 bags of packing peanuts a month. What is the company's monthly profit?

Answer

Goal
Solve for profit

Calculations
Fixed Costs (FC) = Factory Rent + Operational Costs + Administrative Salaries
FC = $6,000 + $1,500 + $4,000 = $11,500

Variable Costs (VC) = Material Costs + Variable Labor Costs
VC = $14 + $4 = $18

Price (P) = $27
Number of Units (Q) = 9,000

Revenue (R) = P * Q = $27 * 9,000 = $243,000
Costs (C) = FC + VC * Q = $11,500 + ($18 * 9,000) = $173,500

Answer
Profit = R – C = $243,000 - $173,500 = $69,500

Hat Profits

A New Jersey company manufactures unique, trendy hats for young adults. They sell each hat for $30 online and in their own retail stores. Each hat costs the company $7 in material costs and $5 in labor costs. The monthly fixed costs include $11,000 for rent and $5,000 in other operational costs. The company sells 12,000 hats a month. What is the company's monthly profit?

Answer

Goal
Solve for profit

Calculations
Fixed Costs (FC) = Rent + Other Operational Costs
FC = $11,000 + $5,000 = $16,000

Variable Costs (VC) = Materials Cost + Labor Costs
VC = $7 + $5 = $12

Price (P) = $30
Number of Units (Q) = 12,000

Revenue (R) = P * Q = $30 * 12,000 = $360,000
Costs (C) = FC + VC * Q = $16,000 + $12 * 12,000 = $160,000

Answer
Profit = R – C = $360,000 – $160,000 = $200,000

Pillowcase Profits

A Washington company sells custom pillowcases. Each pillowcase sells for $25 online. To produce each pillowcase, the company must spend $4.50 on material costs and $7 on labor costs. The company also incurs $2,500 a month on rent and $4,200 on other operating costs like equipment upkeep and advertising. If the company sells 3,000 units a month, what is their monthly profit?

Answer

Goal
Solve for profit

Calculations
Fixed Costs (FC) = Rent + Other Operating Costs
FC = $2,500 + $4,200 = $6,700

Variable Costs (VC) = Material Costs + Labor Costs
VC = $4.50 + $7 =$11.50

Price (P) = $25
Number of Units (Q) = 3,000

Revenue (R) = P * Q = $25 * 3,000 = $75,000
Costs (C) = FC + VC * Q = $6,700 + $11.50 * 3,000 = $41,200

Answer
Profit = R – C = $75,000 - $41,200 = $33,800

Water Bottle Profits

A new company has started producing reusable water bottles. They are selling each bottle for $22 in stores and online. It costs them $7 in material costs and $5 in labor costs to make each bottle. They also have monthly fixed costs of $5,000 for factory rent, $1,500 for machine upkeep, and $3,000 for other operational costs. In month one, they sold 3,500 water bottles. They expect sales to increase by 10% every month.

    a) What is their monthly profit in month one?
    b) What is their monthly profit in month five?

Answer
Part A
Goal

Solve for profit in month one

Calculations

Fixed Costs (FC) = Rent + Machine Upkeep + Other Operational Costs

FC = $5,000 + $1,500 + $3,000 = $9,500

Variable Costs (VC) = Material Costs + Labor Costs

VC = $7 + $5 = $12

Price (P) = $22

Number of Units (Q) = 3,500

Revenue (R) = P * Q = $22 * 3,500 = $77,000

Costs (C) = FC + VC * Q = $9,500 + $12 * 3,500 = $51,500

Answer

Profit = R − C = $77,000 − $51,500 = $25,500

Part B
Goal

Solve for profit in month five

Fixed Costs (FC) = Rent + Machine Upkeep + Other Operational Costs

FC = $5,000 + $1,500 + $3,000 = $9,500

Variable Costs (VC) = Material Costs + Labor Costs

VC = $7 + $5 = $12

Price (P) = $22

Number of Units (Q) = 3,500 * 1.10^4 = 5,124.35 = 5,124 units

Revenue (R) = P * Q = $22 * 5,124 = $112,728
Costs (C) = FC + VC * Q = $9,500 + $12 * 5,124 = $70,988

Answer
Profits = R – C = $112,728 – $70,988 = $41,740

Towel Profits

A textile company sells towels in bulk to hotels. Each towel costs the company $4 in material costs and $2 in labor costs. The company also incurs monthly costs of $7,000 for rent and $5,000 for other operating costs. Since the towels are sold to hotels, the company sells bundles of 200 towels. Each bundle costs $1,600 and the company sells 400 bundles a month. What is their monthly profit?

Answer

Goal
Solve for profit

Calculations
Fixed Costs (FC) = Rent + Other Operating Costs
FC = $7,000 + $5,000 = $12,000

Variable Costs (VC) = Material Costs + Labor Costs
VC = $4 + $2 = $6

Price (P) = Bundle Price / Number of Towels
P = $1,600 / 200 = $8
Number of Units (Q) = Bundles Sold * Number of Towels in a Bundle
Q = 400 * 200 = 80,000

Revenue (R) = P * Q = $8 * 80,000 = $640,000
Costs (C) = FC + VC * Q = $12,000 + $6 * 80,000 = $492,000

Answer
Profit = R − C = $640,000 − $492,000 = $148,000

Chapter 6 Breakeven

Introduction

What are breakeven questions?

Breakeven analysis is the point where revenue received equals the cost of generating that revenue. In equation form, the breakeven formula is:

$$Revenue = Cost$$

Perceptive readers will note that the breakeven equation is derived from the profitability equation:

$$Profit = Revenue - Cost$$

$$Set\ Profit = 0$$

$$0 = Revenue - Cost$$

$$Revenue = Cost$$

Here is an example of a breakeven question:

A running shoe manufacturer sells shoes for $100 a pair. To produce each pair, the company spends $10 in materials and $5 in labor. They have 1 million dollars in monthly operating costs. How many running shoes does the company need to sell each month to breakeven?

Why do interviewers ask these questions?

Like profitability questions, interviewers use breakeven questions to evaluate a candidate's:

- Quantitative skills
- Understanding of business concepts
- Ability to solve ambiguous problems

What are they looking for in an ideal response?

A good answer demonstrates a candidate's:

- Understanding of the breakeven concept
- Ability to explain why breakeven analysis is important
- Aptitude to calculate numbers quickly and use algebra

I expect top candidates to solve breakeven problems in less than five minutes.

How should I approach it?

Breakeven questions are similar to profitability questions, but in the breakeven case, it's about setting profitability equal to zero. Other breakeven-inspired questions may require the candidate to set profitability to a non-zero value.

In either case, use profitability equations to compute the goal, whether it is quantity, price, or cost. For handy reference, here are the profit equations to solve breakeven questions:

- Profits = Revenue – Costs
- Revenue = Price * Quantity
- Costs = Fixed Costs + Variable Costs
- Variable Costs = Cost per Unit * Quantity

Practice Questions

1. A tire factory sells a tire for an average of $200. To produce each tire, the company spends $30 in materials and $40 in labor. They have 3 million dollars in monthly operating costs. How many tires does the factory need to sell each month to breakeven?

2. A manufacturer sells a set of headphones for $300. Material cost is $20. Labor cost is $10. Factory rent is $25,000 per month. Utilities and other operational costs are $10,000 per month. How many headphones would they have to sell to make $7M in monthly profit?

3. A company sells a kitchen knife for $170. Materials for each knife cost $12. Variable labor costs are $5 per knife. Fixed labor costs are $4,000 a month, and factory rent is $13,000 a month. Other operational costs are $9,000 a month. How many knives does the company need to sell to make $6M in monthly profits?

4. A firm sells laundry baskets that are used by college students across the country. They are currently selling each laundry basket for $30. The cost of each laundry basket is $4.50. The rent costs $15,000 a month. Other operational costs are $7,000 a month. If the firm wants to make $800K in monthly profit, how many laundry baskets would they need to sell?

5. A California company manufactures college t-shirts. Their t-shirts sell for $20 at campus stores and $25 online on the manufacturer's website. 60% of their sales come from the campus stores; 40% of their sales come from the website. Each t-shirt costs the manufacturer $3 in material costs and $4 in labor costs. Their fixed costs are $12,000 a month for rent and $3,000 in other operational costs. How many t-shirts does the company need to sell to make a monthly profit of at least $200,000?

6. A local ice cream shop makes novelty ice cream and sells it by the pint. Each pint costs $2 in ingredients and $1 in variable labor costs. They sell each pint for $8. Their monthly fixed costs include $8,000 for rent, $2,500 for operational costs, and $5,000 for administrative salaries. If administrative salaries dropped to $4,000, how many pints would they have to sell if they wanted to make at least $200,000 in monthly profit?

7. A Virginia company manufactures gardening scissors. They sell each scissor for $35 online and in their own retail stores. Each scissor costs the company $5 in material costs and $3 in labor costs. The monthly fixed costs include $17,000 for rent and $8,000 in other operational costs. How many scissors does the company have to sell to make a monthly profit of at least $250,000?

8. A Washington company sells beach umbrellas. Each umbrella sells for $40 online. To produce each umbrella, the company must spend $8 on material costs and $7 on labor costs. The company also incurs $3,500 a month on rent and $6,500 on other operating costs like equipment upkeep and advertising. How many umbrellas does the company need to sell to make at least $150,000 in monthly profit?

9. A Texas company produces TVs. They are selling each TV for $1,100, on average. It costs them $300 in material costs and $50 in labor costs to produce each TV. They also have monthly fixed costs of $750,000 for factory rent, $800,000 for machine upkeep, and $500,000 for other operational costs. How many TVs do they have to sell to make a monthly profit of at least $100,000?

10. A company makes trendy stuffed animals. The stuffed animals sell on average for $50. Each stuffed animal consists of $4 in material costs and $2 in labor costs. The stuffed animals are sold on an online marketplace. The marketplace charges a $50 monthly fee. It also draws a 15% commission for each item sold. The company has additional monthly fixed costs of $15,000. How many stuffed animals do they need to sell to make a monthly profit of $40,000?

11. Domino's Pizza is launching a new seasonal pizza, and the marketing team wants to promote this new pizza during the Super Bowl with four 30 second spots. Your boss asks you, "What ad conversion rate do we need to make the Super Bowl ad to pay off?"

12. After reviewing your calculations from Domino's Pizza I with your colleagues, the finance team suggests that you incorporate ad fatigue your estimates. Ad fatigue is when an ad is shown repeatedly, the conversion rate drops.

Tire Factory Breakeven

A tire factory sells a tire for an average of $200. To produce each tire, the company spends $30 in materials and $40 in labor. They have 3 million dollars in monthly operating costs. How many tires does the factory need to sell each month to breakeven?

Answer

Goal
Solve for quantity (Q)

Calculations
Profit = R − C = $0
R = (P * Q)
C = FC + (VC * Q)
(P * Q) − FC − (VC * Q) = $0

P = $200
VC = $30 + $40 = $70
FC = $3M

$200Q - $3M - $70Q = $0
$130Q - $3M = $0
$130Q = $3M
Q = 3M / $130

Answer
Q ≈ 23.1K tires

Headphones Breakeven

A manufacturer sells a set of headphones for $300. Material cost is $20. Labor cost is $10. Factory rent is $25,000 per month. Utilities and other operational costs are $10,000 per month. How many headphones would they have to sell to make $7M in monthly profit?

Answer

Goal
Solve for units to breakeven (Q)

Calculations
Profit = R – C = $7M
$R = (P * Q)$
$C = FC + (VC * Q)$
$(P * Q) - FC - (VC * Q) = \$7M$

$P = \$300$
$VC = \$20 + \$10 = \$30$
$FC = \$25K + \$10K = \$35k$

$\$300Q - \$35K - \$30Q = \$7M$
$\$300Q - \$30Q = \$7.035M$
$\$270Q = \$7.035M$

Answer
$Q \approx 26{,}056$ headphones

Kitchen Knife Breakeven

A company sells a kitchen knife for $170. Materials for each knife cost $12. Variable labor costs are $5 per knife. Fixed labor costs are $4,000 a month, and factory rent is $13,000 a month. Other operational costs are $9,000 a month.

How many knives does the company need to sell to make $6M in monthly profits?

Answer

Goal
Solve for units to breakeven (Q)

Calculations
Profit = R – C = $6M
R = (P * Q)
C = FC + (VC * Q)
(P * Q) – FC – (VC * Q) = $6M

P = $170
VC = $12 + $5 = $17
FC = $4K + $13K + $9k = $26k

$170Q – $26K – $17Q = $6M
$170Q – $17Q = $6.026M
$153Q = $6.026M

Answer
Q ≈ 39,386 knives

Laundry Basket Breakeven

A firm sells laundry baskets that are used by college students across the country. They are currently selling each laundry basket for $30. The cost of each laundry basket is $4.50. The rent costs $15,000 a month. Other operational costs are $7,000 a month. If the firm wants to make $800K in monthly profit, how many laundry baskets would they need to sell?

Answer

Goal
Solve for units to breakeven (Q)

Calculations
Profit = R − C = $800K

R = (P * Q)

C = FC + (VC * Q)

(P * Q) − FC − (VC * Q) = $800K

P = $30

VC = $4.50

FC = $15K + $7K = $22k

$30Q − $22K − $4.50Q = $800K

$30Q − $4.50Q = $822K

$25.5Q = $822K

Answer
Q ≈ 32.2K laundry baskets

T-Shirt Breakeven

A California company manufactures college t-shirts. Their t-shirts sell for $20 at campus stores and $25 online on the manufacturer's website. 60% of their sales come from the campus stores; 40% of their sales come from the website. Each t-shirt costs the manufacturer $3 in material costs and $4 in labor costs. Their fixed costs are $12,000 a month for rent and $3,000 in other operational costs. How many t-shirts does the company need to sell to make a monthly profit of at least $200,000?

Answer

Goal
Solve for units to breakeven (Q)

Calculations
Monthly Profit = R – C = $200,000
$R = (P * Q)$
$C = FC + (VC * Q)$
$(P * Q) - FC - (VC * Q) = $200,000$

Store Price (SP) = $20
Online Sales Price (OP) = $25
Number of Units Sold in Stores (SQ) = 60% * Q
Number of Units Sold Online (OQ) = 40% * Q
$Q = SQ + OQ$
VC = $3 + $4 = $7
FC = $12,000 + $3,000 = $15,000

$SP * SQ + OP * OQ - FC - VC * Q = $200,000$
$20 * SQ + $25 * OQ - $15,000 - $7 * Q = $200,000$
$20 * (60\% * Q) + $25 * (40\% * Q) - $15,000 - $7 * Q = $200,000$
$12Q + $10Q - $15,000 - $7Q = $200,000$
$15Q = $215,000$

Answer
$Q \approx 14,333$ t-shirts

Ice Cream Breakeven

A local ice cream shop makes novelty ice cream and sells it by the pint. Each pint costs $2 in ingredients and $1 in variable labor costs. They sell each pint for $8.

Their monthly fixed costs include:

- $8,000 for rent
- $2,500 for operational costs
- $5,000 for administrative salaries

If administrative salaries dropped to $4,000, how many pints would they have to sell if they wanted to make at least $200,000 in monthly profit?

Answer

Goal

Solve for units to breakeven (Q)

Calculations

Profit = R − C = $200,000
$R = (P * Q)$
$C = FC + (VC * Q)$
$(P * Q) − FC − (VC * Q) = \$200{,}000$

P = $8
VC = $2 + $1 = $3
FC = $8,000 + $2,500 + $4,000 = $14,500

$8Q − \$14{,}500 − \$3Q = \$200{,}000$
$8Q − \$3Q = \$214{,}500$
$5Q = \$214{,}500$

Answer

Q ≈ 42,900 pints of ice cream

Scissors Breakeven

A Virginia company manufactures gardening scissors. They sell each scissor for $35 online and in their own retail stores. Each scissor costs the company $5 in material costs and $3 in labor costs. The monthly fixed costs include $17,000 for rent and $8,000 in other operational costs. How many scissors does the company have to sell to make a monthly profit of at least $250,000?

Answer

Goal
Solve for units to breakeven (Q)

Calculations
Profit = R – C = $250,000
R = (P * Q)
C = FC + (VC * Q)
(P * Q) – FC – (VC * Q) = $250,000

P = $35
VC = $5 + $3 = $8
FC = $17,000 + $8,000 = $25,000

$35Q – $25,000 – $8Q = $250,000
$35Q – $8Q = $275,000
$27Q = $275,000

Answer
Q ≈ 10,185 scissors

Umbrella Breakeven

A Washington company sells beach umbrellas. Each umbrella sells for $40 online. To produce each umbrella, the company must spend $8 on material costs and $7 on labor costs. The company also incurs $3,500 a month on rent and $6,500 on other operating costs like equipment upkeep and advertising. How many umbrellas does the company need to sell to make at least $150,000 in monthly profit?

Answer

Goal

Solve for units to breakeven (Q)

Calculations

Profit = R – C = $150,000

R = (P * Q)

C = FC + (VC * Q)

(P * Q) – FC – (VC * Q) = $150,000

P = $40

VC = $8 + $7 = $15

FC = $3,500 + $6,500 = $10,000

$40Q - $10,000 - $15Q = $150,000

$40Q - $15Q = $160,000

$25Q = $160,000

Answer

Q = 6,400 umbrellas

TV Breakeven

A Texas company produces TVs. They are selling each TV for $1,100, on average. It costs them $300 in material costs and $50 in labor costs to produce each TV. They also have monthly fixed costs of $750,000 for factory rent, $800,000 for machine upkeep, and $500,000 for other operational costs. How many TVs do they have to sell to monthly profit of at least $100,000?

Answer

Goal
Solve for units to breakeven (Q)

Calculations
Profit = R – C = $100,000
$R = (P * Q)$
$C = FC + (VC * Q)$
$(P * Q) - FC - (VC * Q) = \$100,000$

$P = \$1,100$
$VC = \$300 + \$50 = \$350$
$FC = \$750,000 + \$800,000 + \$500,000 = \$2,050,000$

$\$1,100Q - \$2,050,000 - \$350Q = \$100,000$
$\$1,100Q - \$350Q = \$2,150,000$
$\$750Q = \$2,150,000$

Answer
$Q \approx 2,867$ TVs

Stuffed Animal Breakeven

A company makes trendy stuffed animals. The stuffed animals sell on average for $50. Each stuffed animal consists of $4 in material costs and $2 in labor costs.

The stuffed animals are sold on an online marketplace. The marketplace charges a $50 monthly fee. It also draws a 15% commission for each item sold. The company has additional monthly fixed costs of $15,000.

How many stuffed animals do they need to sell to make a monthly profit of $40,000?

Answer

Goal
Solve for stuffed animals to breakeven (Q)

Calculations
Profit = R – C = $40,000
R = (P * Q)
C = FC + (VC * Q)
(P * Q) – FC – (VC * Q) = $40,000

P = $50
VC = $4 + $2 + $50 * 15% = $13.50
FC = $50 + $15,000 = $15,050

$50Q - $15,050 - $13.50Q = $40,000
$50Q - $13.50Q = $55,050
$36.50Q = $55,050

Answer
Q ≈ 1,508

Domino's Pizza I

Domino's Pizza is launching a new seasonal pizza, and the marketing team wants to promote this new pizza during the Super Bowl with four 30 second spots. Your boss asks you, "What ad conversion rate do we need to make the Super Bowl ad to pay off?"

Some additional information:

- A 30 second Super Bowl spot costs $3.5M. Given the seasonal pizza flavor, this pizza will only be in market for one year.
- In the US, the company owns about 60% of the stores, 40% of the stores are owned by franchisees. For company-owned stores, the cost per pizza sold is 25% of revenue. For franchisee-owned stores, the cost per pizza sold is 95% of revenue because the franchisee pays a 5% license fee to the company.

Answer

Using our assumptions, Domino's Pizza will break even if 0.17% of Super Bowl viewers (approx. 189K viewers) try the new pizza. See below for our calculations.

Goal

Solve ad conversion rate (B) by first solving for the number of pizzas (Q)

Assumptions

Here are some assumptions we are making:

- Price per pizza = $15
- Super Bowl ad reach = 111M people
- Customers that try the pizza and become customers = 90%
- Average number of pizzas purchased per customer = 11.
    - We are assuming that a customer consumes on average 12 pizzas per year. 90% of customers become regular customers and purchase one pizza per month, which is equivalent to 12 per year.
    - The other 10% will only purchase one pizza. After the 1st pizza, they will purchase their 11 remaining pizzas at a competitor's store.
    - Taking these assumptions, the weighted average is 90% * 12 + 10% * 1 = 10.9 pizzas, which we round up to 11 pizzas.

Equations

Here are some equations we will use:

- Profits = Revenue – Costs
- Revenue = Price * Quantity
- Costs = Fixed Costs + Variable Costs
- Variable Costs = Cost per Unit * Quantity

Calculations

Breakeven is when Profits = 0 = Revenue − Cost. Rearranging the equation, we get Revenue = Cost.

Let us start with costs:

- Costs = Fixed Costs + Variable Costs
- The cost of Super Bowl ads is a one-time cost. It's $3.5M per Super Bowl ad * 4 spots = $14M.
- The cost of making each pizza is a variable cost.
- For company-owned stores, cost of goods sold is $15 * 25% = $3.75
- For franchise-owned stores, cost of goods sold is $15 * 95% = $14.25
- The blended cost of goods sold is $3.75 * 60% + $14.25 * 40% = $7.95
- Costs = $14M + $7.95 * Q

Let us go onto revenues:

- Revenues = Price * Q
- Revenues = $15 * Q

To breakeven:

- $14M + $7.95 * Q = $15 * Q
- $14M = $7.05 * Q
- Q = 1.98M pizzas, which is approximately 2M pizzas

Next step, we calculate the necessary conversion rate to sell 2M pizzas. Before we go into calculations, it is useful to think about the conversion funnel conceptually:

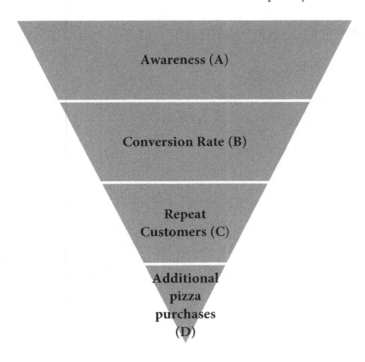

Legend

Label	Description
Awareness (A)	# of people that see the Super Bowl ad
Conversion Rate (B)	% of people convinced to purchase, after seeing the ad
Repeat Customers (C)	% of people who tried the new pizza (as a result of watching the ad) who are willing to buy the pizza again (aka repeat buyers)
Additional pizza purchases (D)	# of additional pizzas that repeat customers purchase

Using this conceptual description, we get the following equations:

- # of pizzas initially purchased (E) = A * B
- # of pizzas additional purchased (F) = A * B * C * D

We will use the following values, either newly assumed or calculated from the first part of the question:

- Awareness (A) = 111M people
- Conversion Rate (B) = Unknown
- Repeat Customers (C) = 90% (new assumption)
- Additional pizza purchases (D) = 11

Working our way through the numbers to solve for B, the conversion rate:

E + F = 2M pizzas

2M pizzas = (A * B) + (A * B * C * D) = (111M * B) + (111M * B * 90% * 11) = 111M * B + 1098.9M * B = 1209.9M * B

Answer
B = 0.17% conversion rate, which is 189K Super Bowl viewers

Domino's Pizza II

After reviewing your calculations from Domino's Pizza I with your colleagues, the finance team suggests that you incorporate ad fatigue your estimates. Ad fatigue is when an ad is shown repeatedly, the conversion rate drops.

The team wants you to model the conversion rate as follows -- 0.4%, 0.2%, and 0.1% -- for the 1st, 2nd and 3rd Super Bowl ads.

Answer

This is an example where you should purchase new commercial spots if the marginal benefit is greater than the marginal cost.

Assumptions

From the previous question, we know the following:

- Number of Super Bowl viewers = 111M
- Profit per pizza = $7.05
- Average pizzas purchased per converted users = 10% * 1 + 90% * 11 = 10
  - 10% of converted users buy 1 pizza and 90% of converted users buy 11 pizzas

Calculation, First Commercial:

Super Bowl viewers (M)	111
Converted rate	0.40%
Converted users (M)	0.444
Average number of pizzas purchased per year	10
Total pizzas purchased (M)	4.44
Profit per pizza	$7.05
Total pizza profits (M)	$31.30
Cost of Super Bowl ad (M)	$3.50
Profit for 1st commercial (M)	$27.80

Answer

Domino's should buy the first commercial spot

Calculation, Second Commercial:

Super Bowl viewers (M)	111
Converted rate	0.20%
Converted users (M)	0.222
Average number of pizzas purchased per year	10
Total pizzas purchased (M)	2.22
Profit per pizza	$7.05
Total pizza profits (M)	$15.65
Cost of Super Bowl ad (M)	$3.50

Profit for 2nd commercial (M)	$12.15

Answer

Domino's should buy the second commercial spot

Calculation, Third Commercial:

Super Bowl viewers (M)	111
Converted rate	0.10%
Converted users (M)	0.111
Average number of pizzas purchased per year	10
Total pizzas purchased (M)	1.11
Profit per pizza	$7.05
Total pizza profits (M)	$7.83
Cost of 3rd Super Bowl ad (M)	$3.50
Profit for the commercial (M)	$4.33

Answer

Domino's should buy the third commercial spot

Chapter 7 Price Elasticity

Introduction

What are price elasticity questions?

Price elasticity is a type of pricing question. Price elasticity is a measure of how demand or supply changes when price changes. Here are some examples:

- Google just launched a new phone, and it retails for $649. Should Google reduce the price by $50?
- Starbucks is considering a latte price increase from $5 to $6. Should Starbucks do it?

Why do interviewers ask these questions?

Price elasticity questions is an opportunity to test a candidate's:

1. Familiarity with business concepts, including profitability, pricing, and elasticity
2. Ability to calculate numbers
3. Recommend a course of action

What are they looking for in an ideal response?

A winning answer shows a candidate's ability to:

1. Describe the price elasticity concept, including what it is and why it is important
2. Apply the concept numerically
3. Make a business recommendation based on the numbers

How should I approach it?

The best way to approach pricing questions is to:

1. Determine the old and the new variables for the price proposal in question including:
   a. Price
   b. COGS
   c. Volume
2. Calculate differences in unit margin and overall gross profit.

When answering price elasticity questions, I have found it helpful to organize information in the table below.

	Old	New
Price	Assume or Ask	Assume or Ask
COGS	Assume or Ask	Assume or Ask
Unit Margin ($)	Calculate	Calculate
Volume	Assume or Ask	Assume or Ask
Gross Profit	Calculate	Calculate

You may also find it faster to calculate volume changes, due to price changes, using a price elasticity factor. Price elasticity is defined as follows:

$$Price\ Elastcity = \frac{\Delta Quantity / Quantity,\ Current}{\Delta Price / Price,\ Current}$$

For the remainder of the book, I will abbreviate the above as follows:

$$E = \frac{\Delta Q / Q}{\Delta P / P}$$

Here is an example of how to use price elasticity: let us say price elasticity for cigarettes, E, is -0.3. That is, for every 1% rise in price you can expect a -0.3% decrease in quantity. If you also happen to have the values for Q, ΔP, and P, then you could easily calculate ΔQ by using algebra, as shown below.

$$E = \frac{\Delta Q / Q}{\Delta P / P}$$

$$-0.3 = \frac{\Delta Q / 300\ million}{2 / 8}$$

$$\Delta Q = -0.3 * \frac{2}{8} * 300\ million = -22.5\ million$$

This means that if a company currently sells 300 million cigarettes at $8 per pack, it can expect sales to drop by 22.5 million if it raises prices $2 to $10 per pack.

Practice Questions

1. Google just launched a new phone, and it retails for $649. Should Google reduce the price by $50?
2. Disney recently released a new Star Wars movie. Should Disney recommend that movie theaters increase Star Wars ticket prices from $8 to $9?
3. Altria, the parent company of Marlboro cigarettes, is considering a Marlboro price increase from $8 to $10 per pack. Should Altria do it?
4. Considering the previous question about Marlboro cigarettes, what price will maximize Altria's sales?
5. Starbucks is considering a latte price increase from $5 to $6. Should Starbucks do it?
6. The price of one-way ticket from Seattle to New York is $400. Should JetBlue raise the price to $450?
7. Would you advise Sam Adams to raise its prices by 10%?

Google Phone

Google just launched a new phone, and it retails for $649. Should Google reduce the price by $50?

Show your work below. Make any assumptions as necessary. Answer on the next page.

Answer

Assumptions

- COGS = $200. Assume it is the same before and after.
- With a $50 price cut, we assume that the units sold will increase from 5M to 6M.

Calculations

Google's Profit from a Revenue Increase

	Old	New
Price	$649	$599
COGS	$200	$200
Unit Margin ($)	$449	$399
Volume	5M	6M
Gross Profit	$2.25 B	$2.39 B

Answer

Google's gross profit will increase from $2.25 B to $2.39 B. Google should go ahead and do the $50 price cut.

Star Wars Ticket Price

Disney recently released a new Star Wars movie. Should Disney recommend that movie theaters increase Star Wars ticket prices from $8 to $9?

Answer
Assumptions

- The movie "Star Wars Episode I: The Phantom Menace" box office was $1.027 billion. For this calculation, assume that the box office sales of the new Star Wars movie will be $1 billion.
- On a big box office movie, Disney, the producer, typically gets 80% of the box office or $800 million in this case.
- For an average movie, the price elasticity is -0.87. However, Star Wars is not an average movie. Star Wars fans are very loyal, so they are likely demand inelastic. Let us assume that demand elasticity is about 10% less than the average movie, or -0.8.
- Assume COGS remains the same before and after the price increase.

Calculations

So, the change in demand will be:

$$E = \frac{(Q - Q_0)/Q_0}{(P - P_0)/P_0}$$

$$-0.8 = \frac{(Q - 125)/125}{(9 - 8)/8}$$

Solving for Q, the new number of tickets will be 112.5 million tickets.

To get movie revenue, multiply the new volume by the new ticket price. Then, multiply that number by 80% to get Disney's share.

Disney's Revenue from a Price Increase

	Old	New
Ticket price	$8	$9
Seats sold	125M	112.5M
Revenue	$1B	$1.012 B
Disney's Revenue Share	**$800M**	**$810M**

Answer

Disney should encourage the price increase because it would increase their revenue from $800M to $810M.

Marlboro Price I

Altria, the parent company of Marlboro cigarettes, is considering a Marlboro price increase from $8 to $10 per pack. Should Altria do it?

Show your work below. Make any assumptions as necessary. Answer on the next page.

Answer

Assumptions

- Last quarter, Altria's revenue for smokeable products was approximately $6 B.
- Marlboro accounted for 40% of those sales or $2.4 B.
- Average price of a Marlboro cigarette pack is $8.
- The price elasticity of cigarettes is approximately -0.3. That is, for every 1% rise in price you can expect a -0.3% decrease in quantity.
- Assume COGS remains the same before and after the price increase.

Calculations

First, we calculate Marlboro's current unit sales:

$$\frac{\$2.4B}{\$8 \ per \ pack} = 300M \ Marlboro \ packs$$

Then, we calculate the volume change:

$$E = \frac{\Delta Q / Q}{\Delta P / P}$$

$$-0.3 = \frac{\Delta Q / 300M}{2/8}$$

$$\Delta Q = 22.5M$$

Therefore, expect sales to drop by 22.5 million packs per quarter because of the increase. The number of packs sold will be 300 – 22.5 = 277.5 million.

To get Marlboro's new revenue, multiply the new volume by the new price. Calculations are summarized below.

Marlboro Revenue from a Price Increase

	Old	New
Marlboro sales	$2.4B	$2.98B
Packs	300M	277.5M
Price	$8	$10
Marlboro sales	**$2.48B**	**$2.78B**

Answer

Marlboro sales will increase from $2.48B to $2.78B. Altria should go ahead and raise the price.

Marlboro Price II

Considering the previous question about Marlboro cigarettes, what price will maximize Altria's sales?

Show your work below. Make any assumptions as necessary. Answer on the next page.

Answer

Calculations

To find the price that maximizes sales, take the first derivative of sales and price and set it to zero. In other words, dSales / dPrice = 0. See below for the calculations.

Start with the following equation: Sales = Price * Quantity

Define P_o as the initial price and Q_0 as the initial sales quantity. Also, define P as the new price and Q as the new sales quantity. Then use the elasticity equation and plug values from the previous question:

$$E = \frac{\Delta Q / Q}{\Delta P / P}$$

$$E = \frac{(Q - Q_0) / Q_0}{(P - P_0) / P_0}$$

$$-0.3 = \frac{(Q - 300) / 300}{(P - 8) / 8}$$

Or Q = 390 – 90P/8

To determine the price that maximizes price is to take the first derivative (dSales/dPrice) and set it to 0:

Sales = P * Q = P * (390 – 90P/8) = 390P – 90P²/8

dSales / dPrice = 390 – 180P / 8

Answer

Set 390 – 180P / 8 = 0 and solving for P, the ideal price is $17.33 per pack.

The following illustration demonstrates how profit fluctuates as price changes:

Marlboro's Profit

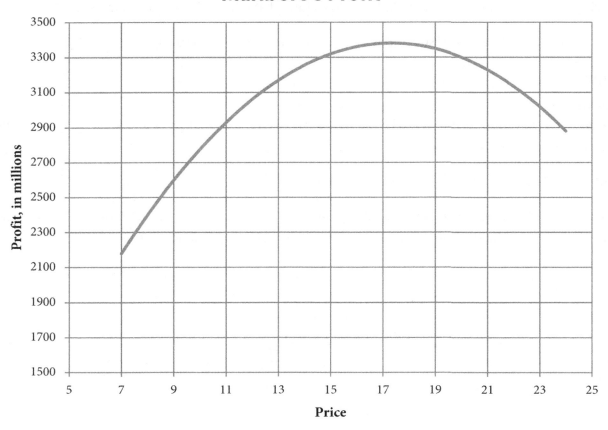

Starbucks Coffee Latte

Starbucks is considering a latte price increase from $5 to $6. Should Starbucks do it?

Answer

Assumptions

Current situation

- Starbucks sells $12.5B in beverages each year.
- 80% of beverage sales or $10B is from coffee-related beverages. It comprises of three product lines:
    1. Lattes are 25% of all coffee-related sales.
    2. Cappuccinos are 25% of all coffee-related sales.
    3. Drip coffees are 50% of all coffee-related sales.
- Lattes, cappuccinos and drip coffee have 80% margins.

New situation

- Latte volume will drop 25% in total, due to the price change.
    - 10% (of total latte volume) will switch to Starbucks' drip coffee.
    - 10% (of total latte volume) will switch to Starbucks' cappuccino.
    - 5% (of total latte volume) will switch to lattes at a non-Starbucks store.
- Margins for lattes, cappuccinos and drip coffee will remain the same.
- Prices for cappuccinos and drip coffee will remain the same.

Calculations

Volume Calculations, Old Scenario

	Old Price	% Total Sales	Old Sales	Old Unit Sales
Latte	$5.00	25%	$2.5B	500M
Drip	$2.50	50%	$5B	2B
Cappuccino	$5.00	25%	$2.5B	500M
Total			**$10B**	**3B**

Volume Calculations, New Scenario

	New Price	Old Unit Sales	Pct. Vol. Change	New Unit Sales
Latte	$6.00	500M	-25%	375M
Drip	$2.50	2B	+2.5%	2.05B
Cappuccino	$5.00	500M	+10%	550M
Total		**3B**		**2.975B**

Profit Calculations, Lattes

	Old	New
Price	$5.00	$6.00
Gross Margin %	80%	80%
Unit Margin ($)	$4.00	$4.80
Volume	500M	375M
Gross Profit	**$2B**	**$1.8B**

Profit Calculations, Drip Coffee

	Old	New
Price	$2.50	$2.50
Gross Margin %	80%	80%
Unit Margin ($)	$2.00	$2.00
Volume	2B	2.05B
Gross Profit	**$4B**	**$4.1B**

Profit Calculations, Cappuccinos

	Old	New
Price	$5.00	$5.00
Gross Margin %	80%	80%
Unit Margin ($)	$4.00	$4.00
Volume	500M	550M
Gross Profit	**$2B**	**$2.2B**

Answer

Profit will increase from $8B to $8.1B. Starbucks should go ahead with the price change. See below for the calculation summary.

Total Gross Profit Impact, Latte Price Change from $5 to $6

	Old	New
Gross Profit, Lattes	$2B	$1.8B
Gross Profit, Drip coffee	$4B	$4.1B
Gross Profit, Cappuccino	$2B	$2.2B
Gross Profit, Total	**$8B**	**$8.1B**

JetBlue

The price of one-way ticket from Seattle to New York is $400. Should JetBlue raise the price to $450?

Data about the company and the flight and the company:

- Operating expense per Available Seat Mile (ASM): $0.116 or approximate to $0.12
  - ASM = # of seats * distance
  - For example, 190 seats * 2,000 miles = 380,000 ASMs
- Average load: 86.2% or approximate to 85%
  - Load refers to the percentage of seats that are sold. The remainder are unsold.
- Distance from Seattle to New York: 2048 miles or approximate to 2000
- Seats per plane: 190, based on an Airbus A321
- Elasticity of long-distance flights is -1.5

Answer

Calculations

First, let's determine the revenue change due to the price increase:

Old Situation

$$Seats\ per\ flight\ (aka\ volume) = 190\ seats * 85\%\ load\ factor = 161.5 \cong 162$$

$$Revenues = 162\ seats\ sold * \$400\ per\ ticket = \$64,800$$

New Situation

The elasticity of demand for long distant flights is -1.5:

$$E = \frac{(Q - Q_0)/Q_0}{(P - P_0)/P_0}$$

$$-1.5 = \frac{(Q - 162)/162}{(450 - 400)/400}$$

Isolating Q:

$$Q = 131.6 \cong 132$$

With information on the new scenario, we can summarize the revenue change from the price increase:

Revenue from a Price Increase

	Old	New
Price per seat	$400	$450
Seats sold	162	132
Revenue	$64,800	$59,400

Now we can calculate the profit from the price increase. Let us first calculate the cost, which will be identical in both scenarios, regardless of how many seats get sold:

$$Total\ cost = ASM * seats * distance = \$0.12\ ASM * 190\ seats * 2{,}000\ miles = \$45{,}600$$

Profit from a Price Increase

	Old	New
Revenue	$64,800	$59,400
Cost	$45,600	$45,600
Profit	**$19,200**	**$13,800**

Answer

Profit decreases from $19,200 to $13,800. JetBlue should not increase the price.

Additional Tip

A more sophisticated way of solving this problem is to create a function of Q as a function of P and calculate the optimum price, subject to the constraint that Q is smaller or equal to 190.

Sam Adams Beer Prices

You have the following data about Sam Adams in millions, unless otherwise specified.

Barrels Sold (thousands)	3,750
Revenues	750
COGS	375
SG&A	62
Advertisement	200
Operating Income	113

The brewer has near certainty that COGS will increase this coming year by 10%, due to unfavorable weather conditions.

Would you advise the brewer to raise its prices by 10% as well?

Answer

Assumptions

- Price elasticity of beer = -0.2.
- SG&A and advertising costs remain the same.

Calculations

Let us start by calculating the price per barrel:

$$Price\ per\ barrel = \frac{\$750M\ revenue}{3,750K\ barrels\ sold} = \$200\ per\ barrel$$

Then, let's solve for the new quantity sold, given the proposed price change:

$$-0.2 = \frac{(Q - Q_0)/Q_0}{(P - P_0)/P_0}$$

$$-0.2 = \frac{(Q - Q_0)/Q_0}{10\%}$$

$$\frac{(Q - 3,750)}{3,750} = 10\% * -0.2$$

$$Q = 3,675$$

Now we can calculate the change in operating income

Operating Income from a Price Change

Data in millions, unless otherwise noted

	Old	New
Barrels (thousands)	3,750	3,675

Price per barrel	$200	$220
Revenues	$750	$808.5
COGS	$375	$412.5
SG&A	$62	$62
Advertisement	$200	$200
Operating income	**$113**	**$134**

Answer

Yes, Sam Adams should raise its prices. Operating income would increase from $113M to $134M.

Chapter 8 Lifetime Value

Introduction

What are lifetime value questions?

Customer lifetime value is the predicted net profit attributed to having a future customer relationship. It is used to determine reasonable costs to acquire new customers.

Why do interviewers ask these questions?

In the past, businesses used return on investment (ROI) to evaluate a new promotion or line of business. Return on investment is usually defined as follows:

$$ROI = \frac{(Gain\ from\ investment - Cost\ of\ Investment)}{Cost\ of\ Investment}$$

Typically, ROI evaluated an investment on a one-time basis. It did not factor recurring purchases from the customer. As a result, customer lifetime value, which does factor in recurring purchases, became a more popular method to determine the net benefit from a businesses' investment activity.

What are they looking for in an ideal response?

When answering questions on customer lifetime value, the interviewer is looking for the following:

1. **Knowledge**. Do you understand the concept? Can you explain it to others?
2. **Formulas and frameworks**. Do you know the formula for calculating customer lifetime value?
3. **Calculations**. Do you have enough numerical savvy to calculate customer lifetime value?
4. **Decision-making**. Can you use your calculation to generate a conclusion and a recommendation on what the business should do?

How should I approach it?

Use the lifetime value analysis framework below.

1. Start with the expected number of years the customer will be with the company (B).
2. Then, calculate the customer value per year (C).
   a. The customer value per year is based on the contribution per sale (D) multiplied by the number of sales per year (E).

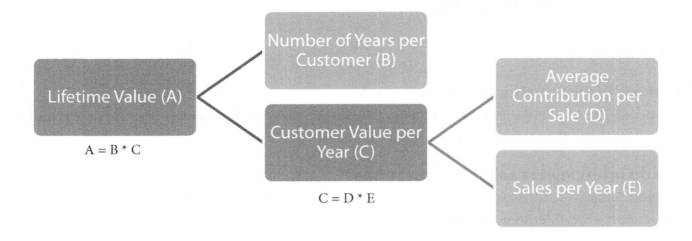

$$A = B * C$$

$$C = D * E$$

If we truncate the lifetime value framework to just B, D and E, we get the following:

$$LTV = B * D * E$$

Practice Questions

1. What is the lifetime value of a Starbucks' customer?
2. What is AT&T's expected profit when a customer buys a new iPhone, with a two-year contract?
3. What is the customer lifetime value of an AMEX card holder?
4. American Express is thinking of dropping its $50 annual fee. Should they do it?
5. What is the customer lifetime value for Crest Toothpaste?
6. What is the customer lifetime value for the New York Times' website?

Starbucks' Lifetime Value

What is the lifetime value of a Starbucks' customer?

Answer

Assumptions

- Average Starbucks customer visits four times a month.
- Average spend per visit is $2.50.
- Starbucks' customer loyalty is 30 years.

Calculations

Use the lifetime value framework, LTV = B * D * E:

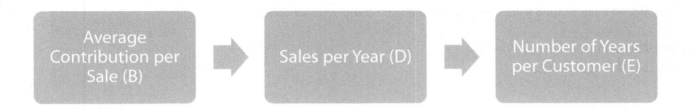

B = $2.50 per visit

D = 4 visits per month * 12 months per year = 48 visits per year

E = 30 years

LTV = $2.50 * 48 * 30 = $3,600

AT&T New iPhone Promotion

What is AT&T's expected profit when a customer buys a new iPhone, with a two-year contract?

Show your work below. Assume that a new iPhone without contract costs $650, but the price goes down to $200 with a new two-year contract. Make any additional assumptions as necessary. Answer on the next page.

Answer

Assumptions

From the given information:

- New iPhone without contract = $650
- New iPhone with two-year contract = $200

We will assume a $70 a month plan and a 55 percent margin on the cell plans. We will also assume that AT&T makes $65 on each iPhone sold, a 10 percent margin on the original $650 retail price.

Calculations

Using the LTV equation:

$LTV = B * D * E$

The LTV calculation includes both one-time revenue and recurring revenue. The one-time revenue comes from the sale of a new iPhone whereas the recurring revenue comes from the cell phone plan.

LTV from hardware, one-time
- B = $200 revenue from phone sale – ($650 * 90%) = -$385
- D = .5 (Purchase one phone every two years)
- E = 2 (Two-year contract)
- LTV from Hardware = $-385 * .5 * 2 = $-385

LTV from cell phone plan, recurring
- B = $70 monthly bill * 55% margin = $38.50
- D = 12 (Pay bill every month)
- E = 2 (Two-year contract)
- LTV from Cell Phone Plan = $38.50 * 12 * 2 = $924

Net LTV
- LTV from Hardware = $-385 * .5 * 2 = $-385

- LTV from Cell Phone Plan = $924
- Total LTV = $-385 + $924 = $539

Answer

Net LTV of each new iPhone customer with two-year contract = $539

American Express I

What is the customer lifetime value of an AMEX card holder?

Answer

Assumptions

American Express has two primary revenue streams:

- **Annual fee.** American Express charges an annual fee of $50.
- **Transaction revenue.** American Express charges on average of 2.5% per transaction. For example, if a consumer purchases $100 from Amazon.com, American Express pays $97.50 to Amazon immediately. American Express then gets $100 from the consumer when they pay in full. This is also called "discount revenue." Discount revenue happens for all transactions.
- **Interest revenue.** Customers who do not pay their bills on time owe interest revenue. AmEx collects interest revenue from 40% of all transactions. The interest fee is roughly $15 for every $500 balance.

American Express has two primary cost drivers:

- **Bad debt.** 1% of all balances never gets paid.
- **Operational expenses.** Operational expenses, such as marketing, customer service and cost of capital, are 90% of discount revenue.

Additional information about American Express customers:

- **Average customer spend** is $1,500 per month.
- **Average churn rate** is 20%.

Calculations

Use the LTV equation:

LTV = B * D * E

(Answer continued on next page)

Calculation: Average Contribution per Month (B)

Revenue, per Month

Annual Fee, pro-rated per month	$	4.17
Transaction Revenue	$	37.50
% Transaction Revenue		2.50%
Interest Revenue	$	18.00
% of balances paying interest		40%
Per $500 balance	$	15.00
Total Revenue, per Month	**$**	**59.67**

Costs, per Month

Bad Debt	$	15.00
Per Balance		1%
Operational Expenses	$	33.75
% of Transaction Revenue		90%
Total Costs, per Month	**$**	**48.75**

Net Contribution

Net Contribution = Revenue – Costs = $59.67 - $48.75 = $10.92 per month (B)

Calculation: Sales per Year (D)

12 months in a year (D)

Calculation: Number of Years per Customer (E)

Customer lifetime = 1 / (Churn rate) = 1 / 20% = 5 years (E)

Answer: Lifetime Value (B * D * E)

Lifetime Value = B * D * E = $10.92 per month * 12 months in a year * 5 years = $655 lifetime value per customer

American Express II

American Express is thinking of dropping its $50 annual fee. Should they do it?

Answer

Assumptions

When the annual fee goes down from $50 to $0, we have two new assumptions:

- Monthly customer spend increases from $1,500 to $2,000.
- Churn rate decreases from 20% to 5%

Calculations

For this question, compare the lifetime value with and without the $50 annual fee. I recall, we calculated the lifetime value for American Express I. For this question, we can take that answer and compare it with the new customer lifetime value.

Given	Old	New
Customer Spend	$1,500	$2,000
Churn Rate	20%	5%

Revenue, per Month	Old		New
Annual Fee, pro-rated per month	$ 4.17	$	-
Transaction Revenue	$ 37.50	$	50.00
% Transaction Revenue	2.50%		2.50%
Interest Revenue	$ 18.00	$	24.00
% of balances paying interest	40%		40%
Per $500 balance	$ 15.00	$	15.00
Total Revenue, per Month	**$ 59.67**	**$**	**74.00**

Costs, per Month	Old		New
Bad Debt	$ 15.00	$	20.00
Per Balance	1%		1%
Operational Expenses	$ 33.75	$	42.50
% of Transaction Revenue	90%		85%
Total Costs, per Month	**$ 48.75**	**$**	**62.50**

Lifetime Value	Old		New
Total Contribution, per Month (B)	$ 10.92	$	11.50
Sales per Year (D)	12		12
Number of Years per Customer (E)	5		20
Cust. Lifetime Value (B * D * E)	**$ 655.00**		**$ 2,760.00**

Answer

We recommend that American Express drop the annual fee, as customer lifetime value goes up from $655 to $2,760.

Crest Toothpaste

What is the customer lifetime value for Crest Toothpaste?

Show your work below and use the following assumptions. Answer is on the next page.

- Contribution margin for toothpaste = 50%
- Toothpaste purchases per year = 5
- Average price per Crest toothpaste = $4
- Average lifetime of a Crest toothpaste customer = 4 years

Answer

Calculations

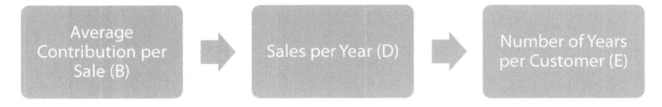

Use the LTV equation, where LTV = B * D * E

Average Contribution per Sale (B)
B = Toothpaste price per sale * contribution margin = $4 * 50% = $2

Sales per Year (D)
D = Toothpaste purchases per year = 5

Number of Years per Customer (E)
E = Lifetime of a Crest toothpaste customer = 4 years

Answer
Calculate the LTV value (B * D * E)
LTV = B * D * E = $2 * 5 * 4 = $40 customer lifetime value of a Crest toothpaste customer

New York Times Website

What is the customer lifetime value for New York Times' website?

Show your work below and use the assumptions below. Answer is on the next page.

Subscribers
- 1% of customers are paying digital subscribers
- 99% of customers are non-paying (free) digital subscribers

Revenue
- Digital subscription fee = $5 per week
- Advertising revenue for paying customers = $0.15 per week
- Advertising revenue for non-paying customers = $0.04 per week
- Contribution margin = 95%

Customer lifetime
- Paying digital customer churn rate = 60%
- Non-paying customer churn rate = 5%

Answer
Calculations

To answer this question, use the LTV equation, where LTV = B * D * E. We will calculate the lifetime value separately for paying vs. non-paying customers:

Paying Customers
Average Contribution per Sale (B)

- Subscription Revenue (B1) = $5 per week
- Advertising Revenue (B2) = $0.15 per week
- Total Revenue (B1 + B2) = $5.15 per week
- Contribution Margin = 95%
- Contribution Revenue per Week = (B1 + B2) * 95% = $5.15 * 95% = $4.89

Sales per Year (D)

- D = Weeks per Year = 52

Number of Years per Customer (E)

- E = Lifetime of a Paying Customer = 1 / Churn Rate = 1 / 60% = 1.67 years

Calculate the LTV value (B * D * E)

- LTV = B * D * E = $4.89 * 52 * 1.67 = $424.65 customer lifetime value of a paying New York Times customer

Non-Paying, Free Customers
Average Contribution per Sale (B)

- Advertising Revenue (B) = $0.04 per week
- Contribution Margin = 95%
- Contribution Revenue per Week = B * 95% = $0.038 per week

Sales per Year (D)

D = Weeks per Year = 52

Number of Years per Customer (E)

E = Lifetime of a Paying Customer = 1 / Churn Rate = 1 / 5% = 20 years

Calculate the LTV value (B * D * E)

LTV = B * D * E = $0.038 * 52 * 20 = $39.52 customer lifetime value of a free New York Times customer

Blended LTV, Paying and Non-Paying Customers
Blended LTV = Percentage of Non-Paying Customers * Non-Paying Customer LTV + Percentage of Paying Customers * Paying Customer TLV = 99% * 39.52 + 1% * 424.65 = $43.37

Chapter 9 Issue Tree Generation

Introduction

What is an issue tree?

An issue tree visually represents a complex issue into smaller, more manageable sub-issues. For instance, this issue tree helps us visualize the sub-issues affecting profitability:

\

We can use this issue tree to explore ways to increase *profits*. The diagram shows that profits can be increased by either increasing *revenues* or decreasing *costs*:

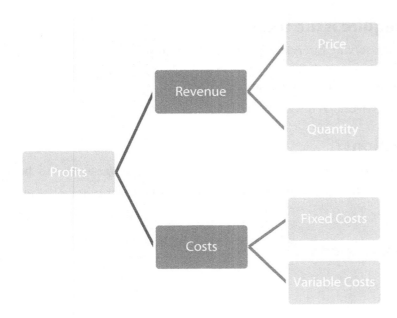

If increasing revenues piqued our interest, we can then explore the two sub-issues that drive revenue increases, which include increases in *prices* or *quantity* of products sold:

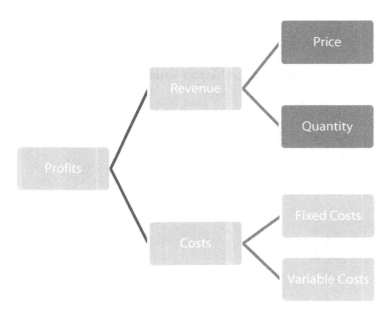

Why do issue trees matter?

An issue tree is an excellent problem-solving and communication tool. Here are some benefits:

- Identifies root cause issues
- Reveals potential solutions
- Easier to follow than listening
- Differentiates from others who don't have visual skills
- Increases credibility by showcasing a logical-thinking process

What kind of interview questions require issue trees?

An issue tree would be appropriate for any problem-solving interview question. For example:

- Diagnose the reasons why McDonald's is not meeting its sales targets.
- Google's traffic is down 7 percent week-over-week. What are the potential causes?

Why do interviewers ask these questions?

On the job, you'll be responsible for solving a myriad of business problems. The interviewer wants to be confident that you have a logical approach to solving that problem, either as an individual contributor or team leader.

What are they looking for in an ideal response?

A good issue tree is:

- Useful

- Logical
- Insightful
- Comprehensive
- Does not contain overlapping issues

How should I approach it?

- **Get the issues out first and organize the tree later**. It's okay if your first draft is a bullet point list of issues. Don't agonize over the fact that it doesn't look like a tree. Just get going. As you iterate, your final product will look more complete.
- **Utilize pre-existing issue trees**. There's no need to re-invent the wheel. For instance, if I'm asked to evaluate why a website's ad revenue is down, I'd start with the basic profitability tree. I'd also memorize the issue tree examples in the Estimation section of this book too; they're excellent starting points.
- **Check that the issues, at each level, are non-overlapping**. In the profit tree example, revenue and costs are non-overlapping. Similarly, if we were to diagnose Amazon.com's product SKUs, we can categorize into physical and digital products, which are also non-overlapping.

Practice Question

1. You own the P&L for McDonald's iconic Big Mac. It's missing its sales target in the U.S. Your boss asks, "How would you diagnose the reasons why we're not meeting our target in the U.S.?"

McDonald's Big Mac

You own the P&L for McDonald's iconic Big Mac. It's missing its sales target in the U.S.

Your boss asks, "How would you diagnose the reasons why we're not meeting our target in the U.S.?"

Answer

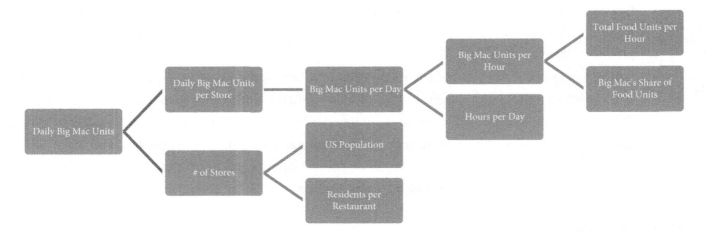

Commentary

- Issue trees, which graphically depict the components of a problem, is an excellent way to diagnose issues.
- We can start by thinking of sales for a single McDonald's store and then multiply by the total number of McDonald's stores across the U.S.
- For a single store, we can think about what drives Big Mac unit sales such as share of total food sales and the hours per day.
- If we'd like, we can augment the diagram above, with additional drivers not shown, that impact Big Mac's share of McDonald's food units including:
  - Price
  - Substitutes
  - Product quality

Chapter 10 Appendix

Common Fractions, Percents, and Decimals

Memorize common fractions; it will be a faster alternative to doing long division.

Rather than do 1428 / 5, know that it is 1428 * 1/5, which is 1428 * .2 = 285.6. For me, it is much easier to multiply by 2 and then move the decimal point over than to divide.

Common Fractions, Percents, and Decimals

Fraction	Percent	Decimal
1	100%	1.0
1/2	50%	0.5
1/3	33.3%	0.33
1/4	25%	0.25
1/5	20%	0.2
1/6	16.6%	0.166
1/7	14.28%	0.1428
1/8	12.5%	0.125
1/9	11.1%	0.111
1/10	10%	0.1
1/11	9.0%	0.09
1/12	8.3%	0.083
1/16	6.25%	0.0625
1/32	3.125%	0.03125

Rule of 72

Rule of 72 is a rule that easily approximates how long it will take for an investment to double. To use this rule, divide 72 by the annual rate of return. For instance, if the rate of return is 2%, it would take 36 years for an investment to double. To further illustrate this rule, we've constructed a table with sample calculations:

Rate of Return	Divide 72 by	Calculation	Est. Num. of Years to Double an Investment
2%	2	= 72 / 2	36 yrs.
3%	3	= 72 / 3	24 yrs.
5%	5	= 72 / 5	14.4 yrs.
7%	7	= 72 / 7	10.3 yrs.
9%	9	= 72 / 9	8.0 yrs.
12%	12	= 72 / 12	6.0 yrs.
25%	25	= 72 / 25	2.9 yrs.
50%	50	= 72 / 50	1.4 yrs.
72%	72	= 72 / 72	1.0 yrs.
100%	100	= 72 / 100	0.7 yrs.

Generally, you'll find Rule of 72 estimates to be precise within one year.

Additional Readings
Other Quantitative Prep Books

150 Most Frequently Asked Questions on Quant Interviews
By Dan Stefanica

Having a strong base of knowledge in finance is imperative in today's business world. This comprehensive book contains questions related to finance, programming, algebra, calculus, statistics, and other topics covered in quantitative interviews. Brainteasers are also included to help build the reader's ability to analyze a problem and find a creative solution. With over 150 questions, this book will keep the avid learner occupied for hours and help candidates ace their quantitative interviews. The answers to the book are practical and flow like they would in an actual interview setting.

Frequently Asked Questions in Quantitative Finance
By Paul Wilmott

Wilmott's quantitative finance book helps finance candidates understand quantitative interview questions and how to ace them. The book contains example questions, critical essays, brainteasers, and common mistakes — all created to guide the reader towards an analytical understanding of quantitative interview questions.

Heard on the Street: Quantitative Questions from Wall Street Job Interviews
By Timothy Falcon Crack

Targeted to aspiring investment bankers, *Heard on the Street* is a comprehensive guide to acing your next interview on Wall Street by finance professor, Timothy Crack. With over 300 questions, *Heard on the Street* covers all topics found in investment banking interviews. This includes non-quantitative and quantitative questions on statistics, logic, and derivatives.

Quant Job Interview Questions and Answers
By Mark Joshi, Nick Denson, and Andrew Downes

Quant Job Interview Questions and Answers provide the practice you need to ace your next quant interview. With over 300 questions, the book covers interview questions that revolve around mathematics, probability, algorithms, and programming. Each question contains comprehensive solutions, a discussion of what the interviewer is looking for, and follow-up questions to impress your interviewer.

Statistics Practice

Fifty Challenging Problems in Probability with Solutions
By Frederick Mosteller

In this book, Professor Mosteller, a statistics professor at Harvard University, engages and teaches the reader how to solve statistics problems. Each question contains a complete solution, helping readers learn valuable techniques in cracking each riddle. Helpful for interview candidates anticipating probability questions in their interview.

Math Fundamentals

Short-Cut Math
By Gerard W. Kelly

Gerard Kelly provides 150 math short-cuts, so you can add, subtract, multiply and divide quickly. You'll feel more comfortable figuring out whether large numbers like 727,648 is divisible by eight, multiply 362 x .5 quickly in your head, and readily calculate the square of 41.

Secrets of Mental Math: The Mathemagician's Guide to Lightning Calculation and Amazing Math Tricks

By Arthur Benjamin and Michael Shermer

The authors share their techniques for mental addition, subtraction, multiplication, and division. You'll be impressed with their tricks and tips for lightning-quick calculations that will impress not only your interviewers but also your friends.

Interview Math on the Job

How to Measure Anything: Finding the Value of Intangibles in Business

By Douglas W. Hubbard

Hubbard builds on the estimation concepts introduced in *Interview Math*. He explains why estimation is vital not just at the interview, but in the workplace. On the job, one may have to:

- Forecast product revenues
- Explain the impact of a new government policy
- Quantify the value of academic research
- Predict an IT project's risk of failure
- Estimate the likelihood of famine in developing countries

Hubbard argues convincingly that anything can be measured, even in uncertain situations. He shares processes, methodologies, techniques, and anecdotes for estimating almost anything. As a bonus, Hubbard's companion website is full of spreadsheets that demonstrate his best practices in quantitative methods.

What's Next

Thanks for reading! However, our journey does not end here. First and foremost, I would love to hear from you. Please send questions, comments, typos, and edits to: lewis@impactinterview.com.

Second, I have two additional resources for you:

- **Sign-up for my newsletter**. I send articles, interview tips and new sample answers that you will find helpful for interview math. Sign-up at www.lewis-lin.com.
- **Find study partners.** Practicing for interview math is less lonely with a partner. Go to our interview practice community, follow the instructions, and find a study partner: bit.ly/lewis-lin-int-community.

Finally, **I have a favor to ask you. Please review the book on Amazon: bit.ly/review-int-math.** Whether you loved or hated the book, your review can help me improve subsequent editions of *Interview Math*.

Book reviews also play an important in promoting my book to a larger audience, which will turn give me a bigger opportunity to create better interview preparation materials for you in the future.

Thank you for reading and reviewing *Interview Math*. May you get your dream job!

Lewis C. Lin

Acknowledgments

I could not have completed this book without Christine Ko and Marcelo Blinder. They drafted and edited significant sections of the book. With their help, they pushed *Interview Math* beyond what I dreamed. I am glad I had a chance to team up with them; they are dedicated, smart, and hardworking. I also wanted to thank Ha Dinh and Lily Gustafson, who contributed new questions to this edition.

Finally, thank you to the generous individuals below. They reviewed the book, providing invaluable input and feedback.

Abbie Austin

Amritraj Khattoi

Bo-Huei Lin

Debapriya Basu

Jeffrey Kohler

Maxine Whitely

Nicole Tang

Pallavi Hukerikar

Paru Taneja

Prasad Nellipudi

Prasad Velamuri

Ran Erez

Sandra Luo

Soumya Patro

Steve Finegan

Suman Puthana

Vinny Pasceri

Xavi Sio

Made in United States
North Haven, CT
04 August 2023